TOBIAS HILL (30 March 1970–26 August 2023) was a British poet, essayist, writer of short stories and novelist. Selected as one of the country's Next Generation poets, shortlisted for the 2004 *Sunday Times* Young Writer of the Year and named by the *TLS* as one of the best young writers in the country, Tobias Hill was one of the leading British writers of his generation. His award-winning collections of poetry are *Year of the Dog*, *Midnight in the City of Clocks*, *Zoo*, and *Nocturne in Chrome & Sunset Yellow*. His fiction has been published to acclaim in many countries.

ALSO BY TOBIAS HILL

POETRY

Year of the Dog (1995)
Midnight in the City of Clocks (1996)
Zoo (1998)
Nocturne in Chrome & Sunset Yellow (2006)

SHORT STORIES

Skin (1997)

NOVELS

Underground (1999)
Love of Stones (2001)
The Cryptographer (2003)
The Hidden (2009)
What Was Promised (2014)

CHILDREN'S FICTION

The Lion Who Ate Everything (2008)

Tobias Hill
Collected Poems

Introducton by
Maura Dooley

CROMER

PUBLISHED BY SALT PUBLISHING 2026

2 4 6 8 10 9 7 5 3 1

Copyright © the Estate of Tobias Hill 1995, 1996, 1998, 2006, 2026
Introduction copyright © Maura Dooley 2025

The moral rights of the author has been asserted under the Copyright,
Designs and Patents Act 1988 to be identified as the author of this work.

*This book is sold subject to the condition that it shall not, by way of
trade or otherwise, be lent, resold, hired out, or otherwise circulated
without the publisher's prior consent in any form of binding or cover
other than that in which it is published and without a similar condition
including this condition being imposed on the subsequent publisher.*

First published in Great Britain in 2026 by
Salt Publishing Ltd
12 Norwich Road, Cromer, NR27 0AX United Kingdom

www.saltpublishing.com

GPSR representative
Matt Parsons matt.parsons@upi2mbooks.hr
UPI-2M PLUS d.o.o., Medulićeva 20, 10000 Zagreb, Croatia

Salt Publishing Limited Reg. No. 5293401

A CIP catalogue record for this book is available from the British Library

ISBN 978 1 78463 375 2 (Paperback edition)

Typeset in Sabon by Salt Publishing

Printed and bound in Great Britain by Clays Ltd, Elcograf S.p.A

Contents

A Note on the Text	ix
Introduction	1

YEAR OF THE DOG (1995)

London Pastoral	9
Close	11
The Mosquito's Opposite	13
Waiting	15
In the Rooms of the Plague House	17
The Secret of Burning Diamonds	19
A Year in Japan	21
Snake Oil	38
Night-Ride, Japan	40
On the Island of Pearls	42
Today the House is Full of Dishcloths	44
Rio in Carnival	46
Dreaming of Home	49
Prelude	50
From the Bullet Train	52
On the Slow Mountain Train	54
Green Tea Cooling	56
Jael	58
The Vampire's Price	60
The Long Road to Silence	62
The Barber's Daughter	64
The Ritual of Making	66
Makondi Sculpture	68

Midnight in the City of Clocks (1996)

I Transit

The City of Clocks	72
Transit	74
Prisons in a Departure Lounge at Midnight	75
One Day in Hiroshima	77
Homesickness	80
Playing Japanese Chess with the Elder Mrs Uchida	81
Sumo Wrestler in Sushi Bar	83
Earthquake, Osaka 1995	84
Three Wishes in a Small Town	85
The Mule and the Rain	87
How to Light Dynamite	89
Flora and the Admiral	91

II Back to the City

New Verses for Clock City Magpies	95
North-West London, 8.15	96
Love Song	98
Broken Bone	100
Playground at 2 a.m.	101
Sheep's Clothing	102
Xenophobia	104
The Woman who Talks to Ezra Pound in Tesco	106
Life Savings	108
Reasons Why	110
Meat	112
July 14th, 10 p.m.	114
The Beekeepers	115
Midnight in the City of Clocks	117

Zoo (1998)

Magnolia Flowers	121
Draining the Grand Union	122
Twelfth Night	124
Sushi	126
Michael the Zoo Keeper	128
The Elephant Girl	130
Closing Time	132
Leonardo's Machines	134
Gibbons in a Northern Spring	137
How to Curse	138
Flora & Fauna	143
Drunk Autumn Midnight below Victoria Embankment	144
The Patron Saint of Prisoners	145
Prospero's Cell	147
Doctor Crippen in Love	149
Lime Light	151
Poem for a North London Wedding	153
Snapshot of an Egotist	155
Self-Portraits by Children	156
Saturday Night Fever	158
A Night in the Room of the Clown	160
Excerpts from a London Zoo Guide Book, 1928	162
The Island of Pumpkins	164
Dowsing with Whalebones	166
A Page of a Guide to a Small Island	168
A Crossroads	170
The Sound of Cages	177
The Pilot in Winter	179
Nightlight	184

Nocturne in Chrome & Sunset Yellow (2006)

From the Diaries of Henry Morgan, Summer 1653	189
Repossession	191
To a Boy on the Underground	195
A Year in London	196
TV Dinner	219
Synthesis	220
Gravity	222
The Gifts	223
The Nightworkers	224
The Orator	226
Amphibians	229
The Lighthouse Keeper's Cat	230
Five Ways of Looking at my Grandfather	232
The Woman Who Likes Standing Under Trees in the Rain	239
Nine in the Morning in the Station Bar	241
Yellow	243
A Bowl of Green Fruit	244
The Wave	245
Horse Chestnuts	247
Summer Late Night Opening	249
Nocturne	252

Appendix

Some Thoughts on Poetry	257
Index of Poem Titles	261
Index of First Lines	265

A Note on the Text

This book gathers together the contents of Tobias Hill's four published full-length collections. Several poems that appeared in *Year of the Dog*, published by The National Poetry Foundation in 1995, were reselected by Hill for his second collection, *Midnight in the City of Clocks*, published a year later by Oxford University Press in 1996. The poems concerned are: 'London Pastoral'; 'Waiting'; 'The Secret of Burning Diamonds'; 'May', 'August', and 'October' from *A Year in Japan*; 'Rio in Carnival'; 'Green Tea Cooling'; 'Jael'; and 'The Barber's Daughter'. In this volume, each of these poems is presented once, located in the part in which they first appeared, and in their original order.

Some minor changes have been made to spelling, hyphenation, and compound words, to avoid confusion for the reader, but where Hill made deliberate use of such devices and, indeed, neologisms, these have been preserved.

CHRISTOPHER HAMILTON-EMERY
Cromer, 2025

Introduction

'When I was eight, I wrote a novel. I wrote my first poem at eleven. I knew that was what I wanted to do'.

Aged twenty-five, in an interview with Kate Bassett for *The Times*, this was how Tobias Hill explained his vocation as a writer.

When a stroke at the age of forty-two cut short his writing life, Tobias Hill had already achieved more than most writers dream of; four collections of poetry, a book for children, a collection of short stories and five novels. His work had brought him recognition in an Eric Gregory Award, a PEN/Macmillan Silver Pen Award, a Betty Trask Award, a shortlisting for the *Sunday Times* Young Writer of the Year Award, selection as one of twenty 'Next Generation Poets' and a wide readership. A. S. Byatt wrote, 'There is no other voice quite like this'. Helen Dunmore, another poet who also became a writer of fiction, reviewing Tobias Hill for *The Observer*, remarked that his first collection was, 'the work of a young man who can scarcely sleep for wanting to see everything.' Like Dunmore, Hill became more widely known as a novelist than as a poet. Yet, poetry, his love for it and commitment to it, was always at the centre of his writing life.

'Writing stories is like going on holiday somewhere odd and exotic, where the physical laws are all slightly skewed. I always like to get home, though. Back to the poetry.'

During his lifetime, the poetry was published in four collections: *Year of the Dog*, *Midnight in the City of Clocks*, *Zoo* and *Nocturne in Chrome and Yellow*.

The *Collected Poems* is made up of those collections, that have remained in print, in various editions, since their publication.

Across these collections, the reader will see Hill's poetry develop. Yet, though the subject matter may shift location, Hill's attention to light and dark, to the strangeness ever-present in the familiar, his talent for surprising imagery, his delight in sensory detail, his regard for the natural world and his compassion for human vulnerability is consistent. His attention changes only in its maturing confidence and precision. The city itself is explored as an ecosystem, its rivers, canals, secret lives and hidden flora glimpsed, most tellingly, in the transformative veil of twilight.

I was fortunate enough to work alongside Tobias a few times at residential writing centres. He was fascinated by humankind, in all our endless variety. I observed his generosity to his students but also his loving regard for human frailty. A sense of that kindness, together with his curiosity, keen and subtle perception and attention to the material world suffuses his poetry.

His debut, *Year of the Dog* (1995), draws richly from his experience of living in Japan, where for several years he taught English. The sequence 'A Year in Japan', is at the heart of the collection, a cycle of poems considering travel and cultural dislocation. Lyrical and meditative, Hill, with the sharp eye of the outsider, records the bullet train, the mountain train, the fish monger's turtles and frogs, and a feeling of wonder at the strangeness of it all.

His second collection, *Midnight in the City of Clocks* (1996), published only a year later, is in two halves, part of the book, 'Transit' contains further poems drawn from time spent in Japan and Brazil but the second half, 'Back to the City', turns to London, Hill's hometown. After time away, Hill sees the city anew, neon-lit but freshly unfamiliar. The poems move between close studies of individuals encountered or observed in the street, to the shadows of history, from 'The Woman who

Talks to Ezra Pound in Tesco' to 'One Day in Hiroshima'. In this collection Hill's cities become haunted, unsettling places.

A few years later and a third collection *Zoo* (1998), is firmly settled in London. Nevertheless, Hill still writes with the cool eye of the onlooker. Written, in part, during his residency at London Zoo, the collection brings together human and animal life, the tension between the wild and the caged, the observer and the observed. Hill is attentive to the ways in which the animal and natural world persist, even thrive, inside the boundaries of the modern city.

By the time of his fourth collection, *Nocturne in Chrome & Sunset Yellow* (2006), Hill's voice has reached a new maturity. Introducing the collection at a reading for Poets&Players in Manchester, Hill remarked, 'It was the book I always wanted to write about London. I spent years trying to write poetry about London and never quite managing it. Partly because it's hard to get a grip on a big city in writing I think, it's constantly in motion'. London dominates the collection, a city in which grit, sweetness and violence, celebration and elegy come together as a kind of glamour. A central sequence, 'A Year in London', the counterbalance to Hill's earlier sequence, 'A Year in Japan', gives the reader a poem for each month, portraits of daily life as the seasons shift and moods change. Here, Hill balances tenderness with realism. Poems such as 'Repossession' are attentive both to the human cost of urban life and the warmth and colour that somehow persist in its midst.

Asked by *The Guardian* whether he had ever imagined another kind of life, Hill replied:

'I thought I could be a doctor ... My grandfather was an anaesthetist and my grandmother a general practitioner. When I was 13, my grandfather gave me his microscope and slides. The slides, especially, attracted me: little slices of lives, and the ends of lives, which he had taken over decades. They hinted at a world which was harsh, dark and intimately human.'

It is, of course, that very same world, 'harsh, dark and intimately human', that the reader sees has so often excited Hill in his verse.

His poetry moves from the strange, or estranged, to the familiar, from the fleeting to the constant. He delights in the overlooked, the uneasy. He employs a kind of sensory brilliance in his attention, particularly, to light and smell.

This new volume of *Collected Poems* gives us, as readers, the opportunity to travel, with Hill himself, across the vivid, urban landscapes of his lived experience, as well as within the sensitive, lyrical, restless borders of his hidden inner world.

In a diary piece, 'Poetry in Motion' in *The Times*, he commented:

'Poetry is an addiction. This is the best thing. There was a time when poetry was called 'The new rock 'n' Roll' (I think that's gardening now or is it cookery?). More recently, poetry became 'The New Sex'. Personally, I'm quite happy for sex to be the new sex and rock to be rock. Poetry does me just fine as it is. And whatever else happens in my life from here on in, I know I've written a few good lines of poetry.'

MAURA DOOLEY
London, 2025

Collected Poems

Year of the Dog (1995)

for Xandra

London Pastoral

There's something I've wanted to show you. Here—
between derelicts:
a bomb-chink of brake-lights.

Ice? More? Just say when.
Open the corrugated paper
of these lung-machine blinds;
sun slides across the floor,
contained as yolk-skin.

Unlock the mortice-lock and pause and swing open
wide windows. Seagulls on the curry-house
scream of distance with the voices
of illegal aliens. Hold onto your fluted glass.

I wanted to tell you something:
for three nights now a bird has sung
in the road trees. A water song.
The neighbours are complaining; no one
knows what species the bird is. No one
even sees it. Pools coupons
titter against chain-links. Chip cartons
scuttle past time-delayed,
time-locked shopfronts. Then the bird
starts to sing.

You'll hear it with the window open,
even when the first rain gathers
to a downpour, hallways sweet
with the residue of road-tar.

Then you can grin, or watch me grin,
at wood pigeons in wet weather
sat in the road trees, suffering
damp white collars. Like divorcees,
not looking at one another.

Close

The cockroaches are rain-skittish.
They run like condensation
from foundation-cracks, stumble and flex
their wings. One flies like a stone.
Grandmother Kamate, pickling white radishes,
claps the beetle to her breast
when it falls there. She mutters, tuts
at the sky. Wipes her loose skin
with a Kleenex, shoos her grandchildren
outside. Tightens her house-kimono, then
opens her *Lucky Strikes* and smokes.

Outside, I sit uncomfortably
by Mr Kim's Nissan, watching
the grandchildren wrestle and sing.
Aeroplanes are disguised as thunder,
thunder as the slop and buckle
of rain in buckets of clouds
waiting for a door to open.
Dogs yip, echo
like dolphin song. Cicadas
rant small rain dances. The smell
of pennies and oysters,

electric. Rain; always gives me
that howling feeling. Times to check
my watch, bus timetables, or
wire Mr Kim's car and drive,

air so close to tender skin
it comes alive, and just behind,
rain creeping like an edge of char
across pages of maps and horizons.

The Mosquito's Opposite

Such a brilliant weapon
spawned from the dull clay-cool of a water jar
or from an oil-lacquered puddle.

Improved to its place like a stone
in a sea. In a ring, faceted. A brilliant thing.

Its blueprint, scribbled in amber,
is unaltered. The conceived form
near-perfect, never improved upon. The line
surer than Picasso's circle, fine
as a shark's teeth, a flatworm's gut,
the unbreakable fractal of a fern.

The vibration of its wings
figures in dreams as the whine
of a dentist's drill, the songs of glass
and the air-raid siren, or
a small child weeping. Alone
and the walls listening.

There's almost nothing to it. Blood,
no heart. The broken drift of legs
under the rubber stomach, where
the forms of life less familiar
latch and grow towards release.

Permanence and its opposite:
the host, the virus antigen

shifting from face to grotesque face
down in the heartbeat of the blood.

Waiting

Before morning I'm waiting here,
drinking green tea by the red door.
In my pocket there are keys,
two pens, one emptied. One of the keys
opens a box in England. In the box
is my grandfather's microscope,

with iris-valves that wink and dilate
like snake-eyes, and chipped glass sides
of a sexless baby's head
small as my watch-face; a foetus—

this is irrelevant. This is
relevant. The night sky

goes down behind Wu's Viking Grill
And Beer Hall. Clouds move
like mountains. I wait.
Across Seven Stone Children Street
the fishmonger's son carries tuna
by the cheeks, hooks up crabs.
He looks them over with the care
of a potter. Sour ash

lifts from the icing factory.
I scribble margin-notes. A bloody rash
of water spreads from the butcher's door.
The match-scratch of the first cicada
ignites the sun. By twelve o'clock

it's a cymbal-crash
in the high branches. My knuckles crack, hands
on the page, waiting to cut
the ventricles and heat of noon
with the tremor of a pen.

In the Rooms of the Plague House

When summer comes, no one is left
to halt the termites' veiny roads
before the bridge the villa doors
and populate the shanty-towns. Nothing is felt
when ribbed dogs fight
for bones under the colonnades
and no one hears the bell-beetles
stringing the dusk with telephones.

The inmates of the fine white house
are gone. There is a rusty smear
of blood the doctors would not touch
where the last carrier was shot.
The daughter, whose honey-black hair
was striped as the hips of a bee,
moves like fish-skin in the harbour.
Phosphorescence haloes her.

Some of them died in secret,
most were killed. Virus excites virus.
Arrangements of flowers and salt
were left inside the airless rooms.
They hide the emergence of rot.
The windows crossed and nailed shut.

Entropy gains momentum. Blood
is split into constituents,
protein, iron, and sold off
to white ants and Red Admirals.
The stink of ozone in the streets

is overcome by the cesspit gas.
The petrol-station creaks under
the whisky-gold dynamite sun,
explodes. The white house is charred black.
The rain steams and polishes it
smooth as a cenotaph's granite.

Inside the multiscreen, left on,
has fused the complicated script
of circuitry behind the walls.
A lithium-cell radio
reports the plague's progress North-East,
the virus already global,
a myth. Discussed but never thought.

The flower vases in the hall
are Edo period and Lalique,
nothing stolen. Nothing touched.
In the infant and child ward,
by trestles, convolvulus
contract,

lungs fighting for breath,
dustless as skin.

In the plague house
the children wait for vaccination,
sitting still, knuckles white.

The Secret of Burning Diamonds

Bought from the marts of Amsterdam
the city built on herring-bones,
where emeralds dug in Ceylon
glittered and still smelt of oysters—

this one was the first to burn,
a diamond ugly and flat—
lustred as a cod's eye. The size
of a black-olive stone, or so,
smelling of mine-mud. Flawed at heart,
the Jews of Rialto gauged it
(their wives and daughters topaz-eyed),
and wouldn't pawn it for a shirt.

Not for the rose-cut, that one, tough
stubborn-ugly. Its chandelier
hatchmarked with cracks and despite that
the strongest substance in the world:
diamond. A lock for alchemists
to break. A Bluebeard's Door, a fear.

A courtyard in Florence. Lenses
and barrels make a microscope
bigger than siege-cannons. The jewel
under the glass, set in steel.

On the clothes of the audience,
a whiff of morning markets, sweat
and pomanders. Cedar, olives,
with branches like green bronze. The sun
rising. Noteworthy men, thinkers,
waiting to vivisect their God
under the momentum of light.

Apex. Strengthening in the lens,
a rift of noon. The diamond
smokes—

wonder! The prince or the Dauphin
whispers profanities. Hisses
of proofs and miracles
and the crack of an atom,
the dam-burst of flame—

a miracle. The purest jewel
reduced to dust.

A Year in Japan

JANUARY

The newspapers, chained to the rack,
could be today's or yesterday's;
I cannot read what day it is.
I sit beside the hotel clock
and watch the certainty of time.

The hotel ashtray-cleaner
brings me green rice-cakes
wrapped in veined leaves.
They smell of fish and nicotine.
Tokyo fills the window's frame.

The towers and the ground-scrapers
excrete vapour and in the rain
a rush-hour of bicycles
threads the stop-lights. The sky is grey,
blank. A dead computer-screen.
The horizon is fused with smog.

A Chinese girl with orange hair
sits cross-legged by the TV.
She channel-surfs. Monsters, baseball,
game shows and samurai blend
into montage, are suddenly lost
in a tide-hiss of static snow.

I wake. Night. A chameleon worm
of subway train turns gold and green
between two love-hotels, burrows
under a Coca-Cola sign.
The traffic's spine of tail-lights
slows by the pinball palaces
where neon dragons leap and dive.

The girl with orange hair is gone.
The computer has come alive.

FEBRUARY

At six my rooms shake when the train
rocks by. Its cables flash and sway
before it comes after it's gone.
Doors swing. The kitchen clock falls like a bomb.

I go looking for coffee,
needing it, and not really knowing
if there is coffee in Japan.
Along the streets, shops are shut up
behind locked grills till ten o'clock.

Only the all-night store's awake,
spilling white neon on the lot
where old men in white pantaloons
sit and chat like radios
in the half-dark, not listening.

Monologues on their past loves.
The fishmonger opens for business.
Lifts the skin off the back of a salmon
with the skill of a killer removing his gloves.

I sit alone in the public garden
drinking coffee from a can,
enjoy its bitterness alone,

listening to the crickets' scratch
like telephones in empty rooms.

March

For my birthday, roast sparrow
and saké from a blue bottle.

Under the concrete viaduct
the white dog of the carpenter
barks into its own echo.

It's market day outside the shrine.
Bruised arcs of prawns and ruddy knots
of octopus. A steel plate
of mullet heads. A wooden tub
of elvers, flexing
and reflexing.

Between the factories and maize
the flowers of the plum ripen
from sapling green to barest hint
of blood. The hunchbacked women work
among the figs, their hammer-blows
a skip before the hammer-beats.

By city hall, salarymen
throw rice at the tail-thrust
and ripple of black carp
in the frozen pool,
echoes in a mirror.

April

Noon. In its sleep the earth turns over
with the ease of eels in a bucket;
oily, muscular. Schoolchildren

brake their bikes. Beside the road a cockerel
cocks his rusted plumes,
goes on digging with his spurs
into garbage. A farmworker
leans on her adze, watches him,
her cheek cuddling chewing-gum.
Grinning. Clothes lacquered smooth with dirt.

My rooms shudder again, when
the couple in the flat upstairs
make love. Once in a month, almost
without a sound. Face to the wall.
He's unemployed. Before lunchtime
he wakes. Lights up. Turns on the news.

A night, lamp-lit zeppelins
roll overhead like harvest moons,
advertising abalone
and rice. I walk with eyes to the ground,
avoiding cracks. Testing the stone.

MAY

Spring in the rush-hour train:
the ticket-man, sumo-fat
and hurrying. The frills of his uniform
confettied with blossom.
Cherry in the hat-band, plum dark
in the splendid epaulettes.

Sunlight blinks between the hulks
of love-hotels. A pyramid, a Palace
of Versailles. Balconies
on the Garden Babylon
backlit, ivy polythene green.

The businessman in the next seat
reads graphic erotica. Holds the book
in both hands. In each strip
vamps and rapes, demons. Thick
as a Shakespeare. He doesn't look
at the girl in the seat opposite,

though I watch her, safely sleeping.
Head back, and the sun filming
her face. How the eyebrows are raised
when she dreams. And beyond her, small
in a landscape of water,

the flash of a kingfisher
taking a clean kill
like a lit crack in carnival glass.

JUNE

After eight days the fall eases.
Roof-tiles shine, blue as a bruise.
The white noise of rain season
stops. Rooks cough in the hush.

The crops are plastered to the mud
like sodden hair against a forehead.
The hammered clods
glazed with white clouds.

Smog begins to gather round
the neon of the gambling halls
and the arc-lights of factories. It tastes of iron,
garlic, burnt, its compound changing on the tongue.

Evening. In the sun's first long gleam
the sky's measure is taken in
by the reach of the rainbow. Schoolboys ride home
against the rising wind, taking their time.
Their girls lean into them, side-saddle.
Wide skirts and black hair
flying. The air glitters with dragonflies.

Hidden by bar-room gloom
I envy them the moment,
jealous of their discoveries.

July

Sweat cools to a sheen
on skin and asphalt.
Gravel as warm as teeth in a mouth.

It stays that way, when the red earth
and troutskin sky register only
as terms of grey. Noon's aftershock.
Street lights wink on, paid out straight
into the street's vanishing-point.

In the calligrapher's backyard,
by yesterday's picked herring-bones,
boulders erode. Their seams of quartz
the white tusks of a mastodon.

Sweat cools. Under my palm
the page spread, and the writing-brush
a teardrop of black ink. I write
the characters for poem, sun.
Foreign and incompetent. Again.
Dip the brush. Rest it light.

Outside, the children play, pollen
from sunflowers and white moth-wings
dulling the darker stains of ink.

Two languages. Characters in
the flue of water and the flow
of limbs. Their language, at their feet.
Words in the script of rooftops, roots,
letters shaped to the fold of a bough.
In dust and the wide eye of the mind,

pages gathered to the path of the wind.

August

Between the rag-slap of docks
and the winch-creak of abattoirs,
she stops talking. In pairs,
alone, the warehouse men
go home. Quiet, faces down.

Later, the saké warm as milk,
she finds the word for them. 'Untouchable.'
'How could you tell?' She rubs her hands,
washing, 'Their bones. Eyes. Differences.'
Their name means *Waste People*. They work
with blood, the filth of animals.

Summer, season of poisonings.
In the space of hours, kept meat
colours, rainbows on asphalt tar.
Eggs are sucked light with hidden rot.
Crack open to a curd of gold.
The fishmonger drinks turtles' blood,
it washes the heart clean and strong;
he recommends it, as he guts.

Evening. Next door a snakeskin hangs
nailed over the window frame, drifts
in the wind. Poison for ghosts
and sickness. The mosquitoes whine.
Quiet, when it comes, is
only the presence of intent.

Down by the docks and abattoirs
the workers sit by the sea-shrine,
dreaming of summer in Japan.
Sweating with slight fever, heads bent,
waiting for the night-shift siren.

SEPTEMBER

Their bodies red as fishing-floats,
dragonflies bask by the outposts
of a US Army base, bunting
strung along perimeters.
In typhoon season the razor-wire,
suspended tight as lute-stings,
shrieks like an accident,
fills the air with its wings.

On Sunday, the fishmonger's window
has been jewelled overnight
with frogs. Duck-neck green, bellied with gold.
They are the last to go, dug back
into thick cauls of paddy-mud.
I wake from dreams of deafness
to the loss of frog-song.

Night has become a quiet time,
the earth a motor cooling, cold.
Bats navigating
on the far edge of sound.

October

She meets the train
at Burning Stone station,
red leaves in her pocket
and the river from the mountain
green as an eye.

The sun keeps rhythm
through the pines. The train beats time. She tells me that
her names translate as Three Eight Sweet One,
Sickle-Hand, and that her town
is famous for carrots, and that

the moon has no face in Japan,
but the shadow of a hare, leapt
from the arms of a god.

Later, under the sod-black trees
she hides her face against the wind
and asks me to teach her to kiss.

November

By the subway exit
the tramp with watchmaker's hands
has gone on his rounds, leaving
three magazines, five blankets, folded small
under the granite statue
of Persephone in Hell.

He's from Beijing. Sometimes he writes
Chinese characters on her breasts.
At eight-fifteen, the rush-hour
bottlenecks, to read the words.

He cleans her skin
himself, rubbing mica flecks
with back-pages of newspaper.
Reads them and then sogs them
in the computerised fountain.
He stands by its corkscrewed chrome,
waiting for water to come
and the snowflakes fat as cornflakes.

I watch him from the park's interior,
behind the temple. No noise
but the slew of a car, the snow's clomp
falling from trees
and from the kindergarten

the sound of mass hysteria.

December

The tranquillity—
no cars. Green soaks
into ice on the traffic-lights,
slithers to red. New Year's Eve,
full of the sound of temple bells.

I cool. She comes late with presents.
Black eyelash, white snow. Ice-cream.
A wrist-watch that glows in the dark
like a moon paralyzed in fullness.

My flight is booked. Tokyo, London.
We eat. We try, now, not to ask
too many questions. At night
she takes my hand in hers and pulls
the quilt over her head, to see.
The time between us, when we kiss.

There are few endings. Death, the twist,
happiness, sadness, Modernist. There are
so few good endings. Now,
snow thaws to rain and falls. The year
ends as the second-hand steps past
in its luminous dark, black
as a wasp's foot. I brew
green tea, drink it and sleep restless,
dreaming of failures, laughter.
Carnival. The Underground.

Four. The dead hour. From the hulk
of Morinaga's Factory
the smell of cooking caramel, its warmth
soft in the cold air and the earth
frozen to asphalt. I walk.
The trees bare, their grasping hands
full of moon's milk.

Snake Oil

Always three steps ahead
of fashion, she wears
reflective contact lenses.
Standing in the mirror's vault
she stares into infinity.
She takes them out only
to screw, but wears them
when she sleeps and dreams.

Along the tendons of her heels
rose tattoos in UV ink.
Later, she'll be dancing barefoot,
the petals lit under strobe lights.
She paints her nails, pouts
snake oil. Plays for another drink.

In the grey trudge of dawn
she slips between the first cars,
teeth on edge with speed, vitamin K,
lock-jawed. She sleeps to ease the hit,
with the white noise of the TV left on.
Sometimes, though her eyes are barred
with mirrors, there will be a word,

a sentence-fragment from the lives
of a watchful family. The slender knives
of silences. Expectations, the lurch
of shame. The hide

and seek. Ten butterflies
trapped without ever knowing
in the summer-house's oven.
She takes their glassy wings,
rouges her cheeks with dead pollen.

A mother's voice calling to church
and the breath of the girl. Running, running.

Night-Ride, Japan

Late-shift done and only the bike
for company. Grease cold, the chain
clanks like a gun factory
and the tundra of rice-fields
page-blank, the snow hardening

to a script of ice. Just here, last night,
the back brake snapped. Popped like a tendon, when
I slewed to watch a star's track, wept
from the blind face of Orion.

Like a firework, but sleet-thin
with distance. At the edge of air.
I tried to wish before it flamed
down to a pebble, out of sight. Rare dust.
Now the dynamo grinds its teeth
and gutters light.

I stop and wait, head back, to catch
snow on the tongue. Its purity
reeks of pollution. Cold oil, essence
of memory. The smell of a tyre-swing
over a river,

a car-crash in Columbia. Cyanide-stench
of gas, burnt rubber. Fish and chips
in a London gutter. Cod-skin,
headline ink and vinegar.

The sky clears
suddenly. Lights wink
up on the radar towers
and the car factories. With one eye
crescent and mad,
Orion stares.

On the Island of Pearls

In memory of Kokichi Mikimoto, inventor of the cultured pearl

Along the jetty, sparrows nag
at the green shells of plum blossom
still clenched, and the sea-sky
luminous as the nape of an abalone.

Something was invented here.
We tour boutiques and show-rooms, where
days are measured out in strands,
their length, lustre. Weeks in the sphere
of one perfect pearl. An organic jewel
that comes in all the colours of the skin.

Something was invented. So many kinds
of failure: the Odd, the Butterfly, the Twin,
which grows into an hourglass.
The Lobe and Tongue, grotesqueries,
worthless. Pain embalming itself like wax
dropped down the candle's shank.
The pearl is a function of pain.

In the next room, a young woman
sits between baroque sculptures;
an ocean shrine, a sea-god's crown
nacred. She bows and demonstrates
the method of insertion,
the oyster's poached skin
slit like the white of an egg. Somewhere
outer doors open, her words
drowned in the sea's yawn and boom.

The jetty smells of white salt, sunshine, plum.
We rest under massive bronze
of the Pearl King. He stands like one, eyes
setting his lands in order
through cataracts of verdigris.
Still looking for the heart, to find
always inside the immaculate pearl

dirt. The lustre of mud.
We buy rice-cakes, walk among
the blossom trees to the arcades,
hoardings on old nails screeching
in the load of the wind. The sound
sweet as bird-song.

Today the House is Full of Dishcloths

Today the house is full of dishcloths,
they pad staircases and loom blue
across back doors, hung out to dry.
The yard cats have got hold of one.
They worry it and leave it scrawled
on the steps like a half-dead bird.

Someone's crying in the hall,
coal-sack eyes pressed against
dishcloths. The kitchen drawers are packed
with four tin-openers and dishcloths
scorch-marked, soft, screen-printed
with Rutland hedgerow birds no one
has ever heard. 'Old Father Thames Hotels'
where none of us have stayed.

At TV dinner time, no one
asks for a serviette. We eat
tin-tray foods, emptying out
the new old freezer in the hall,
with ample dishcloths on our knees.
The house smells of asparagus
and there are small disturbances:

bookshelves cluttered with crocus-bulbs,
allotment onions, 'Pearl' light bulbs,
a glass car ornament, Lalique,
'Swallow drinking', fly-screwed
to a lathed length of boxwood.

Wooden coat-hangers are clumped
on door-knobs. Hung from one, there is
a black waistcoat we all try on,
but which will fit no one. The stairs
are cramped with saucer-tins of film

that tick and burn, unwinding
in a dark room, blazing light.
Catalogued in tight script,
a doctor's time-of-death handwriting—

'Textures'. Tor-grass, mud-ruts, mined
earth. *'Boating'*. The sun's hull, sepia
tide-swells. Snapshots of family,
but always framed from distances.

It's hard to recognise faces.
Harder to search it all and find
this one fine human frailty. Here:
blurred by proximity.

My grandfather's finger
exposed in the foreground.

Rio in Carnival

The earth is hot,
the smell of blacktop
steaming in the rain is sweet
as meat and red lipstick. Coffee
and guarana churn up the guts
into an empty wakefulness.
Roosting in the breadfruit trees
the vultures scent adrenaline,
stretch the blackout of their wings.

Down by Ipanema, the beach
printed with light, curved as a thigh,
Will dances with a transvestite
from Argentina. She sings
Piaf, Marlene and the Stones,
eyes enamelled chrome-blue, too full
of keeping up appearances.

Rain for three days and without sleep,
we drink sugar-cane alcohol
with Mike from Bradford and his girl.
She plays cat's-cradle on his knees, her smile
fixed as the Queen's on watered paper.
'Look at her, see those paps,
young man. Fit as a butcher's dog. Ha!'
Through NHS black spectacles
he winks. Behind his back, the ocean
glitters, thin as caviar.

Women or men? Body-paint runs
blue vines over naked skin.
At the Grand Ball, the beautiful
arrive with godmothers, who watch
not for watchers, the poor voyeurs,
but for the nod, the finger's snap,
the crack of Washington's head on a bill.
In the wings they fix
the price of nights on calculators.

From the upper balconies,
the tourist guides and foreigners
applaud the lambada dancers,
and young bloods bow to the boxes
where old families and new men
observe from the leathered dark.
The band plays music without scores

in the pits, and the view from the gods
inked with the sepia of cigars.

Outside, we find a telephone,
call England. Happy something,
someone. Then wine from the Amazon
in rooms with golden wallpaper.
The liquor cures cancer, and burns—

drums along Copacabana,
dealers and whores working the shades.
Where the sea ends, city begins—

Rio. The mango-man skins fruit
with a machete. Tells us God
took five days to finish this place,
one for the rest. Oil wells up from the soft flesh

and where the shanty-towns have slipped
from the hills in the slough of rain
a body in a ditch of trash
is not a tragedy for most:
death has no more drama
than poverty. Nothing worth waiting for.

Next morning we write postcards home
from the Sugar Loaf mountain
where hummingbirds turn the sun green.

Dreaming of Home

Beyond the rocks of Ephesus
the goatherd led us to a rise
of land over the distant sea;

there were a pair of tesserae,
one gold, one of a fine-grained blue,
disordered in the wind and dust.

There was no crisis there,
there was no heart. The eye searched
for patterns and found only

a lame goat, sheltering
under the steep branches
of the eucalyptus,

a heel bone of the past.

Blood-red seaweeds drip
along that coast—

Not mine. Who wrote this line?
This isn't mine to write—

here. I am here. I am.
The moon is shining
and the frogs are singing.

Prelude

Written in Brazil, 1989

And as the years passed
the first fish,
flashing silver in the bright salt sun
became the fearful glitter of coin
and of the bitter wheeling seagull's eye.
Hunger and pain
and greed.

And as the short years passed
the savagery of the sea,
the rolling of the deep sea,
no longer struck fast fire
from his eyes,
or burnt thick, boiling within his sinewed veins,
but in his ears became
the howling of the thin-ribbed wolf
between cold pines.

And then
the years had passed.
Had ebbed away to the slate sea grey
within his fine blown hair.
The first fish and last
flashed like his sunbright youth
too soon lost and past.

The long years and short,
the green shallows and black deeps
washed away the flame and fire
the fierce desire which burnt but
could not last.

He was left his gaze,
fast across the dawn grey waves
the seagull's scream,
the shipmen's graves.
He was left alone
with the sea.

From the Bullet Train

At the far edge
of the arc-lit terminus
an old man sits in the sunlight
between his backdoor and the tracks,
scooping white pumpkin seeds
from their yellow hollow
with a black lacquer bowl.

Beside me, the businessman's wife
sleeps with her face averted
from her husband or lover,
not quite smiling. Silence
and slow motion. Her eyes open.
The pupils are
pinpoints of thought.

The carriage leans
into the curve of the track,
picking up speed. Zinc roofs
below the viaduct and blue smoke
from the piano factory—
passed in a moment. The sea
levels the horizon.

'Sashimi. Coffee or tea.'
The businessman eats raw eel
from a polystyrene dish
patterned with copper clouds.
I turn. Outside

a swamp town. Sluggish flats
of rice and buckwheat.
A horse and cart.
By its mother's side the colt
running on graceless legs,
learning movement
to the sound of the wheel—

Gone. I sleep and wake only
when the businessman's wife
touches my arm. She points;
bamboo blossom, that flowers
once in every hundred years.

Sallow flowers hung
from a sheaf of spears.

On the Slow Mountain Train

Between the leather seats
the white goat bleats
at the sack that drips
salt water, clicking
with the claws and eyes
of blue crayfish—

'No more room. All clear.'
With mangoes in their teeth,
the children climb the carriages
to ride bareback
across the mountain plain—

'No room!'
Links lock.
Twin tracks.
Mud ruts.
Sunlight.
Women chanting
'Peach, plantain,
plantain, mutton!'
The wheels turn
into themselves.

Ruts of sunlight travelling,
travelling ruts of sunlight

dust. On the old man's lap
a white goose, motionless
under blue hands

that stroke, caress.
Swaying with the carriages.
Stench of alpaca and sweat.

We drink sugar-cane alcohol
that dries the air
until no air is left. He grimaces.
'This is the Devil's Railway.'
The goat-woman, head back, drinking.

'Because it falls from heaven?'
Laughter. He grins
with rusting teeth,
rocking, rocking.

'Because the Devil rides this train.'

Outside, the sky dulls
black smoke
a mane of soot

valiant dust. The crayfish hiss
with pain. Clouds break,
are left broken.
On the mountain plain
we wait for the horizon.

Green Tea Cooling

Noon. In the public park
there is a white scorpion
in the black knuckles
of the cherry tree.
It waits without motion
in a frail cloud of blossom.
The sun trembles
over the yellow grass.

The gardener, buckle-backed
from decades in the rice fields
takes the white scorpion
by its poised tail
smoothly and kills it
on the side of a rock
with the flat of her hand.

'I want to go North.
To Hokkaido. To see the Ainu.'

'Ah, the Ainu. Our natives.
You do not see them
around here in this time.
They are all gone.'

'But in Hokkaido?'

'Perhaps some, in the North.
But here they are all gone.
Like ghosts. Really,
like snow.'

The green tea cools
in our two bowls, as hours pass
in the quiet shade
of the shopfront. Outside
the traffic lessens. Noon

is almost come. The heat
reaches towards
an equilibrium. A white scorpion
waits without motion
in a frail cloud of blossom.

Jael

They came away from our mountain wars
slow with the effort of losing a country.
Foreign men, armour-hulked. Trudging, blood
on their pelts. Outsiders, and that blood
of a different making.

Animals, kneeling to drink, dog-lipped.
Only one cupped his hands and stood. Proud
as the axis lords of Philistine. A leader,
used to strength. Though horses, men and everything
broken in the war's clumsy rout,
half-dead with knock and shield-butt.

Foreign as locusts. Still, I called him
Majesty. Sheltered him, burned olive lamps
when the day grew dim, the shouts
of troops far as Jerusalem
while the clouds skittled rain
over the scree of Ephraim.

He slept here on my bed. No doubt dreamed
of his country. Churches carved
with Baals, green-tongued. His god the demon
of noontide and scorching summers.

After, when Israel had won
its valleys and the high passes
for the goats, the orators made words of me.
They praised the power in my arms, the hands
of a hard worker, though

it was not hard to do. The tent-peg sharp,
sap-tan pine. The mallet solid yew

and he asleep, the cradle-bone
thin at the temples, weak. Lank hair,
the ear full of the road of dream.
To hold the stake, mosquito-soft
and judge the blow.

No work, that—a single breath.
Lighter shift than pressing wine
or camping on the desert plain.
The men gone and the tents to pitch.

No work. I daydream of a king's skull.
My strength, his strength, his death.
And my hands itch.

The Vampire's Price

Ladies and gentlemen, listen!
I won't be stopping here again
for quite some time and time
is precious. Name a price

for this fine ream of paper and
this splendid Tuscan alabaster.
For this brooch, carved from
the eyelid of a whale
and for this Rialto poison.

For this exquisite cat-foot
and for his nocturnal eye
and socket, fitted easily
as gloves—what am I bid? What do I hear

for prescience in fever-dreams? What price,
dear boys and girls, to have
the tungsten of the lungfish heart,
priceless, priceless—

what will I take for skylark-flight?
To catch a swift—like this!
as you might grasp a leaf
from autumn wind, if you are quick:

and how much for this key, wasp-small,
that stops the engines of the mind—
how much, to engineer desire? Pay it.
Pay it as you will.

Have it all. And then,
my love, my vampire,
what will you do for me,
to live forever?

The Long Road to Silence

Only when the green river
between green trees
is left behind us
in its wrought stone

and the wind
sheer and smooth
across worked valley earth
is left

behind and below
can the train halt
on the high plain
between the spread stances
of white mountains.

The small daughter
of the umbrella-maker
brings us tea. We sit
watching the snow-blue moon
falling, without a word
between us.

Thimble-small
the prayer-bell chimes
into a hot noon
without wind;

chimes again,
under the eaves,
thimble of song
filling the distances
between mountains.

Below the dunes
of snow, below this rock
rain ploughs the shining land.
Below this quiet
eagles fly,

eagles fly beneath our feet.
Silence returns
slowly as love. The green tea cools
as we wait.

The Barber's Daughter

With one clean movement
she slides the cutthroat open

with ease, as she would gut
a gulping fish. The foam
she smooths across my cheeks
is wet as sweat.

Her legs are warm
against my arm. 'You shouldn't shave.
You cut yourself. You should come here
always.' The knife
etches my jawline.
In the mirror

the old garage attendant
tipped back in the next chair
watches the small TV
where samurai fight
in a field of snow. Her hand is soft
as the razor. By the door

her grandfather sits in the glare
of neon and sunlight, reading
a comic book. His cheeks hollow
behind the gold dog-teeth.
When she leans close, her hair
covers my heart-beat.
'Grandfather was eaten
by the tiger-sharks
during the war.'

I close my eyes. Her breath
is blossom. Fingers trace
across my neck
and back. The TV
whines and shouts. Beside the door
he turns a page. Red neon
spreads in ripples
over the silence of his face.

The Ritual of Making

'The finest cook in the province!'
her lips whisper
against a spread fan of yen.
The old women, barefoot
at the scrubbed tables
mutter at the show of money.

Over plum tea
and pickled bamboo-root
the customers up at the bar
watch him, the finest cook,
and wait. Around the chopping-board
are white spearheads of cuttlefish,
curlicues of fern and octopus,
crimson and green
in lacquer bowls. At their rims
the black resin
has worn to ochre
under his hands.

The knifepoint drums
against the board.
He rocks with it,
minutely, on the ridges
of his tiny feet. The lockjaw
of a monstrous angler-fish
is folded away smoothly
as a conjuror's trick.
His sunken eyes move to the clock
and back. The oil simmers

towards boiling-point
in a cauldron of clean steel.

'A hundred years old
or more;' my mother says;
it could be true.
I watch the ritual
of his movement. The air
cooks slowly. Outside
the evening grows cold.

Carp pennants
bellying the wind.

Makondi Sculpture

Only the heartwood
of the ebony tree
was used. Only the heart
possesses this lacquer-lustre
and density. Under the hand,
the figure is iron-hard,

bone-thin. Slow hands
and sleepless hunger
translated this figure
from the guttural tongue
of the ebony tree. Only heartwood:
the rest is fused with light
and softness. It has been left
to rot, or burned
under a burning sun.

Hollow as the skeleton
of a vulture and winged
or spread-eagled. The form
is imprecise. Eyeless
or eyed only with axe-strokes
that have left only
blind features. Blind,

hungering, at its ease.
Poised, a hollowed skeleton.
A god of starvation,

blind and waiting.

Midnight in the City of Clocks (1996)

for George, Caroline and Amelia, my family

'Don't spend too much time with nightingales and peacocks.
One is just a voice, the other only colour'—RUMI

1 Transit

The City of Clocks

Slaughter-month. The road is down
and the telephone clacks like knitting.
Departure is set back for days.
To kill the time, we memorise
phrasebook lines, or play mah-jong.
The pieces are made of bamboo
and sealbone, green as oxygen.
We monitor the radio
for facts. The static rises, falls.
I dream of pistons and sirens.

We are returning to the city
where every room has an echo,
each echo, pitch. Whistle right,
and walls thrum like wineglass,
crack. This is where I was born.
I pack a budget travel-guide,
keys and coins, plastic money.

All our maps are obsolete.
Along the oceanside, sinkholes
have cratered the old shopping-malls
with sea-caves, where waves slap like bombs
in the salt dark. The stone arcades
reek of sewage and bladderwrack.

The metro surfaces for this,
follows the racetrack and the ring-road
to an unattended station, lit
with blue Insectocutor light;
moths crack, burned to the metal grid.

This is our destination,
the city of clocks. Block your ears
and you can hear the watches tick
in syncopation with your heart.
No two clocks are ever in time.
If we hold hands, our pulses chat

against one another, like teeth,
gauging the distances we are apart.

Transit

She'd like to sleep. Letters of ice
scrawl a brittle alphabet
on the porthole-glass. Not English, but
a hard, white tongue
like English. She'd like to stop the sky's white noise.
She asks for one more tablet.

The wing is grey and shudders, sharp
as a scissor-blade or its absence
over the sequins of Bangkok's
fast cash and canals and light;
she wants to shred them, cut them out.

In-flight film. In Smoking, lights down,
the man with barcode hair
secretes his hand into her crotch,
snail's pace. Twists it tight.
She's junked-out, her face

crying as she dreams. He sees it;
her mistake. She'll pay for that.
Her tears are beautiful and shaped
like something poisonous; the sacs
of house-scorpions, the wasp's
syringe, the forcep-mouths
of white ants. She dreams

of running, trees. Pines, cage
on cage like helices. Only the earth
unbarred. Like an escape route.

Prisons in a Departure Lounge at Midnight

The man with *Agent of Tai Wing Wa
Hong Kong Lotus Seed Moon Cakes*
printed on his coat is sleeping
on the bench by Duty Free. The cashier
looks the other way, expression
smeared across her cheeks.

He's curved and bunched like an intestine
over arm-rests, covering
shopping bags of caviar.
Around him on the airport floor
tiger-bone salesmen
play for vodka shots. Heads down,
they slap tricks on linoleum
and watch the youngest husband's woman lie back
carved out
eyes shut.

Upstairs in the Mile High Bar,
the night shift air hostess drinks gin with ice,
redraws eye shadows. Waits for flight.
She never licks her lips.
Lights go down in the arcades
where passengers for Ethiopia
sleep flat on newspapers, their plane
delayed for eighty hours.
The washroom shines with clothes hung out
to dry on walls and toilet doors.
An old man reads the Koran, pages
turned to catch the runway lights,
white beard left on like shaving foam.

The smell of acetone exhaustion
stains the plastic café seats
where thirty children sulk and cough
and cabin crews hand out ice-water,
jigsaws of Red Square at Noon,
posters to be coloured in,
500,000 Air Miles To be Won

Only the Duty Free is lit all night.
The cashier with blue cheekbones
behind the cage-block shutters, watching
seven televisions, listening
to Metal, headphones on.

I sit near to the moon cake man
where I can hear the smallbone crack
of screwtop bottles in her hands, and when
she half-sings, out of tune—

She turns, turns, trying selves.
Curls the furs against her thighs.
Outside, the hulks of aeroplanes
begin to move. She watches them
through high windows. Not stopping,
walking round and around the steel shelves.

One Day in Hiroshima

HIROSHIMA NOON

Peace Park. In the postwar trees
cicadas warm up like chainsaws.
The schoolchildren are out to catch them,
insect-cages on their arms
like handbags. Red plastic, green plastic.
Crowding up to reach the noise.

Nothing is happening today.
Watches are reaching noon
on the wrists of lunchbreak men.

There is a sound of aeroplanes
and the small creak of lawn-sprinklers.
Woods the horsemeat salesman
dozes on an iron bench, nylon legs splayed apart.

His slip-on shoes are getting wet.
Sun ticks off the grass as steam,
smoke, the smell of minerals.
He dreams of spring. Teeming rain.
Across the road in the petrol station

borders of hydrangea
bruise against the air, their fists
delicate as litmus paper.
Testing subsoil and heat
for acid and its violence.

Hiroshima Midnight

River town. Ghettos of mud
run out to the sea-roads
between the park of cenotaphs,
the statue to dead high-school girls,
the street of love-hotels. Night brings out
their addiction to the light.

Knuckles raw as pickled plums,
Mister Fatboy pours us out
cold rice wine. We have the same job.
We make money. That's our job.
The barclock in the Gourmet Globe
has stopped. I'm dying for a drink
again. I watch the late-shift cook

skin spring chicken like a glove.
Tomorrow is Day of the Dead, when
all her ancestors ride home
on the curved backs of eggplants.
She hears them now, their insistence
rattling the storm windows.
She washes up, watching the street
for fast cars. Gullwings, tailfins.
Brakelights shimmy along the tram tracks,
asphalt radiating heat
and the lost dog-feet of litter
skittering up Peace Street.

Down by the docks, where the jetsam is,
the summer fireworks begin before we can get through the crowd.
The dark is fused with a smell like zinc;
beer cans and fried octopus. Office men with redmeat faces
splay under the gingko trees,
waiting for the festival.
All along the waterfront, lights in water like barcodes.
The child running through the crowd in summer gown and Adidas
is overhung with fireworks.
She cranes, head back, to watch their fall,
their drift. Spectacles of smoke
flashlit, huge in the mid-dark.

Closing-time. Through my shoes
the road is still warm, and the air
against my eyes and teeth is dry
with gunpowder and river-dust.
Up near the Peace Dome's fairground skeleton,
someone is shouting at someone,

I can't understand what. Mister Fatboy
starts to cry. I help him home,
streets emptied out
with the smell of ozone
and the sepia of streetlights in each dark room.

Homesickness

Beyond the rocks of Ephesus
the goatherd led us to a rise
of land over the distant sea.

There were a pair of tesserae,
one gold, one of a fine-grained blue,
disordered in the wind and dust.

There was no crisis there,
there was no heart. The eye searched
for patterns, and found only

a lame goat, sheltering
under the steep branches
of a eucalyptus,

Heelbone of the past.

*Blood-red seaweeds drip
along that coast—*

Not mine. Who wrote this line?
This is not mine to write—

Here. I am here. I am.
The moon is shining
and the frogs are singing.

Playing Japanese Chess with the Elder Mrs Uchida

Between the ebb of dusk
and turn of night, mosquitoes
gentle as thistledown
alight from the violet air
and settle on my hands and in her hair.
She brushes them away, and mutters
at the choice of pawn or knight.

The wind across the dry field
carries the chinks of bats
like jewels. The coolness
forces us inside. The board
set on tatami mats. She opens windows,
loosens nets. Outside
the rice-farmers burn scrub
to stubble. Mars and Sirius
are dulled, and the moon
ages with dust. She sits.

'My husband is dead.'
'I'm sorry.
How old was he?'

Over the board, her eyes
predict, calculate. Her hands
are veined and livered,
tapping at a pawn
and moving on.
'He is dead.'

'We were married in Autumn.
We say *"Autumn, when
the sky is high
and the horses getting fat".*'
'What did he do?'
'He bought me red cicadas.
Closed in his hands, like this.

Like little birds. They sang
Me-me-.' Her smile works
against the drawn lines
of her features.

Taps, taps. Lancer. King.
'Now he is dead. The cicadas
will not sing again. Ever
ever.' The sky
accumulates darkness.

Sumo Wrestler in Sushi Bar

One salmon-egg, a boil or pearl,
sticks to his doll-lips. He presses it
flat with his elephant fingertips.

Licks it. The barclock is too thin
between minutes, and the floor-mat
learns flatness under his weight.
His thighs flop down like sunstruck apes.

The bulbed light of light-bulbs
illuminates a world born small
and weak, measured in niggling strips
of sour rice and naked turbot.

It leaves him speechless. When he gapes
he redefines the planet with
the head-width of a halibut,

inch-cuts of raw sardine
converted into shoals of sweat.
He orders in his little voice, then waits
for the submarine girth of a bluefin.

Earthquake, Osaka 1995

She leans the door against a wall.
Takes off her shoes. On the freezer is a bottle
of *Plum Orchard Fine Rice Wine*. In the freezer
is the smell of rice fused to clinker in a pot.
Next to the freezer is a hole.
Through it she can see the street:

a boy in shorts is selling cans of Coke.
A boy in jeans is drinking head-down to a puddle.
Between sirens, an old woman
is catching locusts with her hands
in an allotment of tea-green rice.

She wants to help them but the television
has been broken and her arm
hurts to the bone. She pours rice wine
into her mouth, up to the hard brim of her teeth.

It tastes of sour milk.
She fills a cup until meniscus
shivers like clockwork at the brink.

Three Wishes in a Small Town

All day the hills smell of sawdust.
It makes him think of English girls
while he works the cork trees,
stripping them to the red wood:
white-shoes white-handbag-girls
waiting outside Cádiz hotels
with mouths that taste of cigarettes.
He knows their small-talk and their skins,
where they're smooth and where they're broken.

Now tonight his hands smell yellow with sawdust,
like the mouths of smokers.
He wipes them dry and drinks his thirst,
his thoughts, then his direction-sense,

watching the navigation-lights along the coast
of Africa. Listening to expatriates
talking down their homesickness;
the sheep as white as cricketers,
the cast-iron of clouds, and it's
long past midnight, while streetcats ooze like tar
between the fountain and the statue to the Civil War.

He drinks with them until they're gone,
then walks alone to the low-tide mark.
His feet on sand print watered light
between the wormcasts and seagulls.

He likes it here, where nothing talks.
He dreams of catching monkfish by their seabed gills
and when he wakes, his vomit tastes of salt and pearls.

The waves are seamed with light. He feels
clean. Cleaned-out
like gutted fish. The sand is warm. He'd give it all to eat
a plate of eggs. Their yolks and whites and shells.

The Mule and the Rain

I've been watching it all day
while the ice chimes odd times in my gin.
Waiting for something to happen.
In the field by the white hut

the mule is standing on hot bone
hooves. The trees around the house
are heavy with green oranges
and the cold belled clink of the goats
finding roots under the branches.

Siesta. Empty hills the colour
of grape-must, animal shit,
car-yard rust. The mule is propped,
shadow down between its feet,
on sage grass yellowed as the skin of a meat-eater.

An old man in a flat cap, barefoot,
strings up red peppers to dry
on the walls of the white hut.
The wind disturbs them. Nothing else
moves. The mule leans its head out
so that the bones hold their weight.

I don't know what I'm looking at.
A mongrel, punched-black horse standing
all day without moving to eat,
not drinking. It's like watching tides
turning out, the way exposure
cures it like leather. The sun
breaking sweat across its back.

Midnight. I wake half-drunk from dreams of drought
to the low tide smell of wet concrete,
rain churning in the carob trees.
I stand outside, under the eaves,
listening to the sigh of it,
and from the white hut, the sound of grieving,
on and on in the clarity of the night.

How to Light Dynamite

Mr Toumbi's second son, fire slopping from his hand,
throws an Easter cherry-bomb and runs. His flip-flops slap applause.
Crowds thicken in the streets. The air
is clear enough that bat-wings clap
loud as kid-gloves, shaken out.

The father pours out ouzo shots. Bottle-tin
clicks on glass. And all the time he's muttering.
I find it hard to make it out. He says his oldest granddaughter
was buried without hands. He asks
'You know how to light dynamite?'

Good Friday, and all afternoon
sea-foam cooks in the harbour-mouth.
Mrs Toumbi guts white squid, fries them into wedding-rings,
moves with drinks between old men
until they straighten and go home. Over the moorings,
rockets bloom. The sea is cooling like a stone.

'You know how to light dynamite?'
'No.' He wipes his face. Lights up.
His fingers smell of aniseed
and household poisons. The match smokes
like a thurible
in the half dark. 'Like this.'

Cigarette in his teeth,
fist clenched against the wince of ash.
Eyes clenched. 'Like this. To get the heat.
I never knew she smoked. They buried her

without hands.' Outside,
the sea shakes with a noise
like train-tracks. From the hills, the young town men
throw sparklers of dynamite.
The air is spiced with it. The town cistern
leans back and splits its sides.

The sky is turning sepia
with rock-dust. In the flashlit square
people dance and fall dancing,
debris on their clothes and faces.

Mrs Toumbi finds a glass,
sits with us. We drink until
the evening is almost silent
the merlins bat-hunting
over the navigation-point of Venus.

Flora and the Admiral

She keeps the knick-knacks clean like fruit
stacked fresh in a shop-front; shells sour
with brass and gunpowder,
apricot-sized barnacles,
sealed tins of cigarettes. At night,

drinking, not drunk, he sits
hard-backed in the hard-backed chair.
Circling the window's square,
he's pitched into the long head sea, rails
swept under greeny walls. His mouth is watertight.

Flora dusts, listening
to shipping forecasts. German Bight,
Maas Lightship, Scapa Flow. The Admiral
sees tall ships in emptied bottles.
He thinks of them like cathedrals,
lifeworks. The chiselled tongue of a saint
finished by the father's son.
Clinker-built to ironclad. Flora's standing,
back to the wall. He takes her in
like a pin-up unrolled in a mess-room.

She's watching how his body's aged
out of itself. Eyebrows hung clumped
like samphire, breath
in love with salt, skin oilskin, night-sweat
a synthesisation of tar

which she swabs at, smelling on him
the sweet tang of deck-iron
kettle-hot under heavy fire.

But breakfast's the time for remembering,

the kitchen window wide to hills
packed blue-green with cabbages, or
tide-swells, frosted with rain

or his young hands, scrubbed of brine,
pulling her down into a pond of bluebells.

11 Back to the City

New Verses for Clock City Magpies

Eight for black, nine for white.
Ten for a step and its echo at night.
Eleven for credit, twelve for cash.
Thirteen for pickpockets milling the crush.

Fourteen for blackmail, fifteen for tax.
Sixteen for passion in cul-de-sacs.
Seventeen steps from the porch to the car.
Eighteen for life, with good behaviour.

Nineteen pounds ninety-nine pence-ful of lager.
Twenty plus tips for a blow and a popper.
Twenty-one faces pressed flat to the window.
Twenty-two magpies half-lost in shadow.

One for white, two for black.
Three chances left to guess why they attack.

North-West London, 8.15

It's closing time at the bloodmobile.
The oldest Camden derelict
still waits outside for chocolate,
her dirty-old-man coat and smile

lovely as a pub-crawl while she dreams of blood and peppermint.
She doesn't notice when the medic
locks the doors and drives away. She looks up from the pavement
at clouds the size of Regent's Park
and London's fourteen-hour sunset.

She's walking in her head between
Ten Bells, The Green Man and Blade Bone,
their smells and noise; extractor fans,
Special Tonite chuck steak satay,
the burn of Whiskey Flake Rubbed Ready,

velvet rooms stained blue with smoke
like fish tanks, where the couples grumble
together like grindstones
over the minutes of last trains
out into silences and evenings.

She gets as far as Venus No. 5
Off-Licence, Kentish Town. The steps are cold
but when she sits
still, over the taste of gin and rooftops
she can hear the chains
and see the cagework mountain outline

of Lord Snowdon's Aviary
where pelicans and sacred ibis
wink awake their ink-drop eyes
at every key that doesn't fit
each brake light and every footstep
in the dead ends of Water Lane and Haven Street.

Love Song

Promise me something. Promise me
a kiss. Your lips are Methedrine,
faster than alcohol. Swear on
the ram-raiders, the joyriders
garbaging up the night. Swear on
the Underground-surfers. Kiss me.

Come to me in the high places.
Kite Hill and the housing estates
where pensioners behind their lace
wait for your movements and your face.
Let them watch you come to me.

I love the roll of your sex
when you walk, and the black
of your belly after the talk.
Clearness of acts in the quick of the dark.

Show me your skin. Show me again.
Your clothes undone, your nakedness
and eyes open. Watching my face
for lust. Staring, their whiteness
makes my heart beat
you make my heart beat
by the whites of your eyes.

I touch your tears and have no words.
We crouch like borstal cases in stairwells
and cul-de-sacs. Your head back,
your throat open and no more

to give. Hands knotted in my hair. The stars
not burning down on us
like the songs of kings,
only burning. We make our own songs.

Broken Bone

Today the world is ugly:
through Holloway and Kentish Town
the bike bag-lady is riding
with a fish tank on her knees.
In the fish tank is a bone.
She stops outside the library.
She talks the snarl of wind in kitestring.

The world is ugly. The sky
looks like it cut the liver out
and burnt it. Days are when I get
like this. I need a friend all right, but
real friendship is rare. You must know that.

Today is Moss Side, yesterday
was North of Sunset. When I walk
I'm thinking of the girls who look
like something on a chocolate box.
Very chocolate. Chocolate milk.
I'm thinking of spring chicken skin,
peeling off like satin gloves.
Broken bone grinds its teeth
with my footsteps, quick slow quick.

Stop. The third house on the left
has caught my drift again. Sit down.
She's left the upstairs window open.
The fleshy chambers of my heart
wince ash like a cigarette.

The worst thing is how much I love the pain.

Playground at 2 a.m.

What else are net curtains for?
Look. At least switch off the lights.
Call me a poet, call me a voyeur.
Behind the backs of mortgaged flats

the bulbs inside the lamp-post lamps are dark
as onions, and the playground dark
as the places between cities. Inch
the curtains open. There's the bench,

the swings, the wince of cigarettes,
their singe. Close your eyes, let them adjust.
Children are playing on the roundabouts.
You see? Fast hands, his denims down, her breast.

It's not exactly sexual, watching;
It's not exactly not.
Maybe it's a sex assault,
maybe it's remembrance,
to watch her face, his eyes. To try
and catch their features in my fingers.
Press your face against the glass;

they won't notice. Don't be shy,
everyone gets like this sometimes.
It's a kind of fear, it's something
to do with being us,

stopped in mid-step, unwatched, watching
where the action is.

Sheep's Clothing

'May God protect the lamb from the wolf'
—Spanish traditional hymn

Don't get me wrong. Your face is smooth and soft
as clingfilm. But, my love, your voice has claws

and though (quite naturally) I'm pleased to say
that your fine hands do not resemble paws

there is a sweet, dark perfume on your breath
and I find I believe that it has teeth

—In many ways you look like death
warmed up. What is it that you keep

wound up, behind the puzzle-depth
of eyes that are so smiling bright?

I think there's wolf in your sheep's clothing,
but you wear the clothing well.

Come out with me. The city smells
of terrace cakes in terrace houses,
rented rooms and private halls,

the mathematics of small lives; a point
is that which can't be split,
a lifeline is length without breadth—

Will you come out with me? Tonight
the Underground shakes the pavement
and the moon is a heart's-width.

Xenophobia

Lock the door. Is it locked?
When he's trying to get in,
he waits outside the door, the black man,
close as shadow to a foot.

Come in, if you're going to.
Not from round here, are you?
Don't know it. Different street.
Did you get my order? Meat
goes underneath the fly-net. Milk?
Make us up a drink.

Mary. Without blood.
And my binoculars—
Don't think that I can't see, because
I can. Bring them here, if you could.

Do me a favour, jink the curtain back
a bit, to get the park
in. That's where the girls are.
Look at the way they walk, outsiders,
balancing themselves all day
against the whole sky—

I like binoculars, it's good
to focus in slowly. It means
you know where you are by the distance.
But don't look up, or you'll go blind.

Sometimes, when the chair is set
too close to the window, sunlight
warms my feet. I don't like how it
slides between my toes like egg-yolk.
I sit well back. Wait for dark.

I go out when I have to. Out.
Limbs trail from my brain like roots
uprooted from their element.
There's lots to see here. Silhouettes

precise in a dark room, casements
cross-referencing distant walls.
And there are always people out there,
old children. Daffodils
white as searchlights in the gloom.
Children circling to get home. That's their problem,

not mine. I'm home. I've measured it. I'm sure.
There's the spindled chain of the wind-chime,
its bell-shadow touching the foot of the door.

The Woman who Talks to Ezra Pound in Tesco

The woman who talks to Ezra Pound in Tesco
wants to know which bleach works best
to kill off mice in pipes. Pound doesn't know,
and the cashiers look past

her bulk and noise. She's taken down
five kinds of bleach, and now she can't
put them back up, because the dog
—curled prawn-like in her shopping-bag—won't wait,
and gets attacked alone.

Outside, semi-automatic cars
misfire in the suntraps of streets.
I help her with bottles. Today
she tells me to fuck off, they're hers.
Less often, recently, she waits
for recognition, then hugs me, calls me
lovely wee thing, so that I walk home
smelling of old piss, but thankful.

Today she tells me to fuck off.
I carry the dog anyway. It lolls its tongue
through the plastic bag handle.
She holds my arm for safekeeping.

'Have you read my poems? Listen. 'Christ,
and when I sleep/ Your wounds hop on to me
Like little mice . . .' Do you know Mr Pound?'

I tell her no. An ice-cream van unwinds
between the tenements. Net curtains
dislodge screes of dust. A Bluebird, wheelblocked,
creaks in the heat and basks in rust.

Life Savings

The dead worry me.
My hands shake until I scrawl them
into balls of waste paper
stuffed in the bottoms of pockets.
I'm older than my father.
I keep cash and receipts in separate wallets.

Four cans of Guinness, one of
Ambrosia creamed rice. Potatoes.
One lottery card. Nineteen,
thirteen, seven, three, three,
one.

Not all the best things here are free.
The girl who wraps my spuds in Sun
is London Indian Ugandan.
Teeth like radishes.
She marks up vegetables and fruit,
Asps, *Obes*, *Qus*. I could
stand to watch all day. I could.
But the day's getting on.

I don't mind paying. I don't hate
waiting to foot the bill, just
this mountain bike wheel, U-locked
next to the bus-stop all winter.
Spokes clipped, gears crowed out.
Nothing left except the tyre.
Unpunctured, still locked.

Here's the eyehole of my door,
here's the one easy chair.
I know what happens here and what

the cost will be. The carriage-clock, seeding
inside its greenhouse,

the grain-click of seconds.
I don't miss one. I can't listen. I keep the TV on.

After tea I crack a can,
wait for the morning programme.

Reasons Why

Watch this—
Nothing in this hand, nothing
in this hand. In both hands,
something from nothing:

a poem, a wobble of bubble
pulled from the hoop
of a mouth or
from air-pressure

! Here. Eyes wide, look: blossom is
yoghurt-dollops, how it drips
petal-drops. Woodpecker is
a wooden ruler, plucked against
a wooden desk. This is a promise,

given and not kept—a riddle,
slapstick, scratch-and-sniff: bluebells
are fusepaper, gunpowdering
shadows of trees that snarl with traps
of kite-string. Words and silences
will fit to anything and lock
like indexes and thumbs in prayer
or stripes and grass-skin on a liger.

Tigering the pages, lines
printed deep as X-ray burns
or light as ripples in vanilla—

Why? Don't ask me why. Or ask why Les,
the next-door taxi-driver,
stole his wife a goldfish-bowl—
sized gaslight off Buckingham Palace.

Meat

She has another fall at Christmas.
It's while she's ironing,
and she remembers it because
the ironing-board falls on the phone.
Cracks the mouthpiece. Inside
she finds a wasp in the nest of wiring.
Yellow as a high-voltage warning.
Pressed in through the holes
to sleep. Sleepy. She holds it in her hand,
closes the hand into a fist.
It helps her concentrate.

She buys offcuts
and cuts them small,
breakfast, dinner and tea. That way
she gets to watch the box and eat
without missing the London sports.
But cutting's getting difficult.
She uses kitchen scissors first,
to snicker through the raw meat.

Small things go wrong
when they can. It's not senility,
the taps left choking
hot phlegm in dark rooms. The washing
piling up like nasty thoughts.
It all gets lost if she lets it. Pills especially.
It's just that she's got other things
to think about. One other thing.

King's Cross. Mice wince
between the tracks. She leans against
a tube-map. Listens for four-letter words. Watches
a pregnant woman sitting down,
smiling as the load eases. Bitch,
the bitch. She holds in her pain
like mouthfuls of paraffin.

Locks her teeth. If she gives in
it'll escape as laughter, then
ignite the city. No one moves.
Headphones hiss. Her knuckles crack.
There is a watchtick in her head,
a fuse inching towards its dynamite.

July 14th, 10 p.m.

The moon round as an oven-dial.
Ten fire-engines slide their red trombones
up past the Cock and Bottle
and the brink-lights of petrol-stations.

Behind windshields, linked by fax,
Neighbourhood Watch is watching me at work.
I'm looking for the depth of ink
to plus or minus hands or feet. I've found it in the index
of the Central Urban Zone Phonebook:

Jewson, Butler, Brick Lane, Skinner,
Butcher, E17. Blackborn, Blackburn, Black
stock, Market Place St. White City Under
takers, Inc. Rooks clot the branching hemispheres

of plane trees, and the London sky
confused with stagelight and small allergens.
I've lost the point again
of Indus mud in indigo, and the fear of lights-out

in blacklistings. On my side of the window,
a tentacle's shank and a goat's eye
retreat over sandbars and pages.
Or advance. It's hard to tell.
I can't hear a thing in the sirens' shadow.

The Beekeepers

Mr Salter walks across the garden like an astronaut;
washing-up gloves, white net suit.
Something has got inside the gloves.
He puts the slats of honey down, peels
pink rubber to the sting, the bee
looking for weaknesses.
He kills it when it gets upset.

The kitchen floor linoleum
is varnished with old wax. Our shoes
click like fingers. Mrs Salter
closes doors and net curtains.
Insects tumble at the windows,
bees the colour of honey,
wood the colour of honey
the air set yellow with the smell of it.

Outside, helicopters drone
over London. Mr Salter
peels wax from the comb
neat as appleskin. The slough
dropped away to show the bright
shine of something stolen, something

sweet and implicit with gain.
Mrs Salter makes tea,
butters cake, licks her thumb
clean of bittersweetness. Calm
holds us in its amber deadweight.
Mrs Salter pours for us;

she's mother here. My stomach growls. On her lap,
honey drips into the jar,
collecting dark. Transparency,
translucent now. Opaque.

Midnight in the City of Clocks

April, and this year April is
election month. In Rust Belt rooms
we wait for conditions and terms, the dark lit
television-blue. Wind rhymes along the thin tongues
of aerials and nothing moves outside except

downpour. But it's getting late.
I head down through the empty lots
of outbuildings, asphalt road wet
as hair plastered to a forehead.
In the Underground I find
tomorrow's newspapers and sit,
reading candidate predictions and the list
of polling stations. When there's nothing left to read
I try to sleep to kill the time
until midnight, when all the clocks
groan in their mainsprings with the need
for Summertime and difference.

I wake up to a car alarm. The station
coughs with subsidence.
The pavements hiss like fusepaper

and pouring from the ghettos, rain
acid as slag, and with it men
who live out of suitcases, men
who sleep with nylon suits pressed flat
under one-night mattresses.
All around the church clocktowers
the air shudders with hours.

Zoo (1998)

for Hannah, with love

Magnolia Flowers

In the dark
light bulbs are opening.

The cats are out
hunting for blackbirds
through the green earthwires
of long grasses.

The trees are slight.
They are weighed down with blackbirds
which drink the sound of water
out of white bowls.

The water is cold and sweet
with magnolia pollen.
The mouths of the blackbirds
burn with it
like fuse-wires.

The cats hunt what they can.
The sight of burning mouths,
the sound of spilt water.

Draining the Grand Union

It happens quite suddenly,
the engineers doing their work
in the way important work is always done,

with no one noticing, until they've gone
and the canal with them. Its cold green
miles emptied quietly

as a gutter is emptied of rain.
The Grand Union Canal
has been removed, and left behind

are the skeletons of bicycles—
without wheels, without rust—
and twenty years of traffic cones
swollen, sheltering mussel shells
and torn-up letters, and lost coins

blackened or green with oxygen.
In the suntrap of a shopping trolley
an eel has worked its muscle
into soft brown knots
and died under the eyes of children
who watch its eyes turn into moons.

Behind the ten-foot doors
of the lock gates,
canal from here to Manchester
waits to find its level,

forcing green water
through the hinged black wood,

exploring in slow sheets
down old beams and bitumen.
There is the sour smell
of sun below the waterline

where a small man in pink Marigolds
rummages in the mud's cupboards.
Behind his back
the canal waits. Drips

drops. And up above,
a pair of tan-black dogs
watch it all from the footbridge,

their long, simple heads
full of the smell and the bright
shine of undiscovered country.

Twelfth Night

It is a warm winter this year.
The snow comes down as rain
and in your father's house

butterflies hang from the walls.
Scraps of pearskin lacquer
laid thin
across the cold of windows
and the dark arms of furniture.

Open a door
and they shift and dither
with the odd ends of paperchains.

For twelve nights we have been drinking
warm alcohol. Your father talks
of snow leopards escaped from zoos.
Uncle Joe's Minty Balls.
Ice Fairs and the rising seas
and winter butterflies.

They have been salted away
in hard chrysalids
the shape of green almonds

and now they are cracked open,
the world outside is
closed down under the rain.

Nothing here is meant for them.
A radio in the next room,
half tuned in. A pendulum

drowsing. Your father talking
of last June
in his whisky voice.
The way light fell between two bridges
on the Grand Union Canal,

wedged into the green surface.
As if the softness of light
and the density of water
had altered quietly as weather,
green hardening into glass.

Sushi

In the small hours
we eat sushi with our fingers.
It is a cold night
outside, and traffic
lights up the ceiling

in passing. On your skin
is the smell
of sweet abalone,
sweat, and ark shell, and bluefin.

You are picking
red salmon eggs
from white rice
carefully,
like a child with a chocolate biscuit.

On your palms
you warm the eggs,
their soft red pearls.

You break them open—
their skins are so tender—
with the tip of your tongue.

It is a warm night
and my heart is skipping
along, skipping
along—

I would kiss you,
but this is a time to remember
and first I will watch you

eating, and your grin
quick in the dark. I'm getting it clear,

so when I cast my mind back here
it will come skipping,
like a flat stone across flat water.

Michael the Zoo Keeper

His mother was a magician at nights,
pulling rabbits from a *Christy's* hat
after day shifts at Lillywhites,

Crouch End. For breakfasts, she cooked
dove egg omelettes.
He misses their paleness

in missing her. Cleaning cages
and the cells of the elephants
he remembers
the feel of her rabbit hat,
the fur felt
fine as the hands of night mammals,

fine as the hands of the dying.
It is past autumn, and in daylight
the gutters are still filled with the old
seeds of plane trees,
yellow as lionskin.

Now it is darker
and the zoo trees are bare.
Starlings glitter
in their hollow networks.

Darkness concentrates the senses.
Walking home, Michael
smells animals on his skin.
The sweat of the oryx
and the dry eyes of vultures

carried out with him, over
the tarred black water
of the Grand Union Canal
into the city streets

like contraband. Like magic charms.
A monkey paw, a rabbit's foot.
Cheap magic. The moon is out
and pale as a dove egg

to light him home.
He wraps his thin hands
round sweet tea and hot china

then lies awake, listening
for the wolves in their long cages,
for the chirr
of locusts in the reptile house,

all that is close and familiar.
He falls asleep before
the bored cough of a jaguar
echoes down Haven Street.

In the morning
there is snow falling
as he tunes through radio static,
waiting for first light.

The Elephant Girl

1

She forgets her own smell. She tries and can't
catch it. It is the way that she loses
the faces of friends, the streets of places.
Her hair and skin reek of rank elephant.

For sugar, Eve and Martha will fall down
like earthworks in the man-roar of the ring.
Their skin is grey and rough as pumice stone.
It chafes her fishnet thighs. She is smiling.

Two shows a night, and afterwards the tent
tugs and vents the wind over east London
and the elephant cells. Their tusks are gone.
Cut out. If they chose, nothing could prevent

the sum of their grey force. They are holed bones
in Moore's bronzes. The seamed mass of oceans.

2

She thinks them patchwork—
love handles. The soles of feet.
Nubs of fingerprints.

3

She dreams of chess.
The lathed pieces

turn under her horned palms
into the figures of new games.

Worked fossils of mice.
White frogs. The volutes
of seashells.

If she tries
she knows the rules
for the icons of lambs
and the movement of elephants.

The squares stink
of circuses. Small cells.
Butane. Adrenaline

and loss. Over this, hands move.
Touch-move.
The black rooks look like
bareback girls

and the horse totems
whisper, then couple themselves.

Closing Time

For ten days there is no weather
but fog. The air

pressed
into white slabs of mist.
I go for late night milk

out into the thick of it,
my ears ringing with the cold,
taking small breaths

and small footsteps. The roads
have lost their lengths and breadths

in cells of fog, and the pavements
are sluiced down with it,
dark as riverbeds.

The all-night shop is open,
its plaque of light
falling into the empty street

and I buy milk and greenback bacon
and walk home along the green
underpass of the canal.
My hands full
inside each cool pocket.

This is waiting weather.
The moon and the cars
go with slow care
through nothing towards nowhere

and home is further than I thought.
I put the milk
down on the black pavement,
feeling in the white dark
for the edge of keys

and south of here, the Zoo klaxon
begins to sound. Hours late
for closing time. The cry of it looming

through the enclosures of fog,
between the empty aviaries
of the ravens, and the ruined
tenements and alleyways

and the blue shark in its lit tank,
turning and turning back
without rest or impatience or surprise.

Leonardo's Machines

We're waiting for the light to change
and you are reading borrowed books.

The hinges of paperbacks
are held apart on your knees

and your hands
cradle the furred spines.
All day we have been arguing

about nothing. About each other.
Outside the birds are singing,

and the city lights already on.
You put Caesar's *The Civil War*
down by your feet,
with *How to Cook
a Wolf.* Open *Leonardo's Machines*,

turning the pages
as the light turns green.
There is Da Vinci's system
for walking on water
and his device for weighing air,

their line and shade
on smooth paper.
Page ten shows the facsimiles
of weapon forms derived from fruit.
xiv; the helmet-mask.
xvi; the oven-flower.

There is blood on my tongue
or just the taste of it.
There's nothing like the head-butt

of words, their thoughtful violence.
Now your hands are sleepwalking,
knuckles softening out

as the traffic crawls down Brewer Street.
Outside the door of GIRLS GIRLS GIRLS
waits a man in rabbit fur

worn thin, and a woman
in the warm brown leather
of her lover,

both faint in the faint light
as Leonardo's diagrams,

gorgeous and violent as dreams.
'If necessary,
I will build
mortars and light ordinance
with beautiful and useful shapes—'

the hand inventing,
in black chalk,
a way of drawing shadowed ice
or a foetus in the uterus.
The way of putting together
an oil-press. Machines of war

to end war. Moveable fountains.
A mechanical lion
with its chest opening
crammed with lilies—

*'A will be young fir,
which has fibre
and is light. B will be fustian
and feathers. C will be starched taffeta
and for the trial you will use
thin paper—'*

Your voice quiet. The car
louder. The sounds of you and it and us

not going far. Tonight
we won't make love or argument.
This is a quiet time. Look up and out.

Aeroplanes, sleek as guns,
are turning west into the light
and the air over the terraced streets
mutters at the miracle of flight.

Gibbons in a Northern Spring

Under the rain
the zoo enclosures
rust and drip
like shark cages.

The lions are awake,
smelling the reek of ibis
in the sieves of aviaries,

watching the plane trees
sodden and darken
in patterns of giraffe skin.

All day there is no sound but this,
the breath and boredom of lions
sullen as limestone,

the chirrup of traffic lights
turning green in empty streets,

and the gibbons
howling for a yellow noon
in their cages of rain.

How to Curse

1 INGREDIENTS

Take time. Take out the brunt
force of *Jesus fucking cunt.*

For the cursing to go right
strip the mouth down to meat

and say nothing, and drink alone
on balconies, in waiting-rooms

that smell of hotplate coffee burnt
dry and sweet. Lick at your words, like salt.

Grin and your lips will split.
You come from the islands
where people do not lose their tempers;

they almost lose their tempers.
Lose nothing. Keep the lid down flat
on your own stinking pot.
Grin until you see the bone.

Save yourself. Choose your heart.
A pound of muscle laced with blood

works, or a lovebird in its cage
of ribs—what I mean to say is

hate with a lover's care and love
in company and absences.
To curse right, love your enemy.

2 FIELDWORK

Look for violence
everywhere, and you'll find it
everywhere. In the chip-chop
echo of yards and building sites,

in the magpie who talks to the rock-drills,
    in the greenstick
    fracture
of sunlight through inches of glass.

In cities when the lights come on
and the starlings mass in flight,
settling and unsettling.
Their glitter and chatter. Hate can do that.

Wait on this seat in this public place
(where I remember her,
    where I remember her
    sweet talk and sweet small-talk—)

and look for studies in hatred.
There is a man who whispers
spittle and curses to the trees
which only listen, never talk,

which only breathe. And there is one
with her left hand in her right hand,
waiting for lovers, and finding

only the leaves around her,
welts of gold on the grey pavement.

She is waiting to find anything
to say. A greeting; a movement

of lips. Her fingers caged with hate.
Waiting to be promised something.

3 Curse

Promise me you won't forget,
and I'll promise something slight,

that all your journeys will be my journey
where no one stands waiting
at your stations

that all your homes will be my home
where the clock tick
seeds its age into your bones

Promise me you won't forget
and I'll promise what you'll get;

that looking for evening air
or space alone, or someone there
under the red night of cities,
windows and river-lights laid out
like cut stone on a jeweller's cloth—

all you will find is distances
a fear of falling,
a need to run. Only

I remember, you are leant laughing
at an open window
shooing away pigeons
that croo like lovemaking

remember I will still be here.
I promise I'll never forget
the deadbeat of your heart
in the dark,
the belling of your laughter there.
Remember that I won't forget
and you will always have my fear.

4 BREATHING

When the cursing is all done
when the words are made and gone
don't go yet. Wait and sit

in the midpoint of the night
while the day and new day join
and the far coordinates

of the starlights gently turn
let the heat of hatred burn
out into the breathless space

sit in the heart's pause
while the moon loses its light
and the dawn is weak as thought

all around the rim of earth
softly sit and softly laugh
for the freedom and the dearth

where the hatred used to writhe
let the hatred be a wreath.

Close your eyes on all of this and breathe.

Flora & Fauna

Outside the station,
trees dense with green oranges.
I put down my case.

Birds try to settle
around the early street lights.
I'm hungry for fish.

Monday, at first light:
the subway stairwell flooded
smooth for ten minutes

and wind underground.
I turn back for the reek
of human hair.

Drunk Autumn Midnight below Victoria Embankment

And the sky wet as a loose tarpaulin.
I'm walking but not home.

I'm taking the air. It tastes
sweet, like rust. The tide is out

and the mud is thick as meat
over the inner city's chalk.

Here are the broken finger bones
of clay pipes. Traffic cones. The imprint

of my own feet, walking back.
Here is a seed stained black.

Live as a fist, but all I want
is somewhere to sit down a minute,

tomorrow's newspaper (the pages
hot with fish and vinegar)

and the watermark of London sky
green as old money all over the river.

The Patron Saint of Prisoners

There have been better years.
In late August, forest fires

eat through the locust trees,
the beehives burning in neat pyres

of sweet ash. When the meerschaum mine
lays off two hundred men,

The Oyu Zoo is ordered shut,
on grounds of luxury. The stepped

concrete of the wolves' enclosure
is earmarked for an outdoor theatre,

and the camel is auctioned off
in seven shares of fur and rough

topside. The aquarium stock
is given out in Oil Sellers' Park

to anyone who wants it.
Blue angel-fish and the white

ammonite curls of conch meat
spit and blurt in hot fat,

and the ostrich from the aviary
lasts until St Leonard's day

in November—the patron saint
of prisoners and fruit markets.
In the winter streets,

rabbit fat is cheap,
and cardamom and sugar beet

sell at the price of better things,
the town sick of the taste of meat.

Prospero's Cell

The whorehouses and warehouses
of munificent Milan
ring with cash and industry
behind their locks and doors.

In the Street of the Land of the Flies
and the Street of the Lamb
loiterers unlock hard grins

of gold (and gold is hard as trade)
to drink to him, the Exiled Duke,
under a sky
broken with flags.

They don't care that the freelancers still talk
of heresies. A stave, a book.
Witches won't drown, and nor will Dukes
is what some say, or they say

At least he is a Christian,
the man exiled to thirst and sea-salt
guilt-marked by fulfilled punishment,
like Griglié, the demagogue,
who has no tongue to tell his lies.

—The feasts of saints are kept,
and trade by land and sea is good.
Better than good (they say his blood
is white with impotence, his feet
always naked, and all he says is *Where is my cell? Where
is my daughter?*)—

Hidden by laws and tapestries,
the Duke grows old. A little man,
salt skin and an artist's hands.

Nothing to do. Nothing to say
of city-states—of Burgundy,
ransomed by the Arabic
for twelve white falcons
brought from the islands of sea-ivory—

Nothing to him. His voice is
latitudes, distances,
empty aisles of libraries.
The stained light of Venetian glass
stains his face with what he sees—

He sees the retch of storms and words. The island
in itself. The ocean's plow and sow.
The talk of a daughter drowned by wind.
Something said there, not caught, and still to know.

Doctor Crippen in Love

After work he feeds the wolves
in Regent's Park. Keeping his gloves

buttoned, and his fingers clean.
Giraffes with swimming-pool skin

move through the tenements and trees.
One of the wolves has china eyes,

or so it sometimes seems to him. Keen
whites, and blue-glaze irises—

dollybird eyes. He keeps his sleeves
free of her teeth, and watches
until the late spring light is gone.
All of them understand themselves.

There is more time on Sunday,
when he will pay the entrance fee

for the Zoological Gardens
to watch Cuban solenodons
poisoning lizards, or to read
under the green roofs of the reptile house.

Then church. Seven rows in front,
a baby quacks and clucks
in the pale echo-chamber
of morning service.

It stares up at the high windows
where a pigeon is landing,
the grey fingers of its wings

bent back, the innards settling
inside the warmish cage of bones,
the fine sponge of its perfect marrow.

He could explain all that,
would have someone to listen,
if he could. All day is time to kill, and time

to think of love. He eats his tea alone
in Archway, then starts walking

home. Outside the dark shop windows
strings of laburnum flowers
catch the street light above him,
and in its lamp, the light bulb stutters
and stuts like a Geiger counter.

He looks up. Past the bulbs and flowers
glitter Sirius and Mars,

thin with smog. He starts to walk again.
He'd go a long way, to see perfect stars.

Lime Light

There is subsidence.
My father would have hated this,
the groan and the green slump
of the chainsaw's work.

Under the lime tree, white roots
inch their tips
into the sump
of spring rain.
The walls and weight of houses
sink into their white branches.

It's an ugly tree
and it always has been.
The bark is warted black
as London brick
and a bag from Safeways
fluts and pops in the maze
of cut-up logs, twigs and limbs.

Years ago, the trunk
split open with rot.
My father spent two days
painting it with treacle skins
of creosote. I'm also there,

watching from the kitchen door.
Small. The brush strokes
are spare. Out in the sun he grins,
half with pleasure,
half with effort.

Now the tree surgeons
rock at the stump,
twisting it out.
And it comes. A rotten tooth
already dead. Tall as a man

and heavier. Under the black
pocked skin of the lime

the wood is white
as roots. It is barely spring;

there's not much green
or right in this. The tree is gone.

The black hole waits
to be filled in,

and the rooms of the house
alter to what is left of us,
full of a new and unexpected light.

Poem for a North London Wedding

for Patrick & Anna

North London suits them
as they suit one another,
down to the ground and the hopscotch game
faint on the asphalt. Late-night laughter

between terraces built to last
in 1890. Shopfronts stacked

with armfuls of green sugar-canes,
thighs of yam, and figurines

of ginger. Ghetto blaster drivers
booming north past Whitehorn Flowers

('Bridal Bouquets at Short Notice')
and the Kapetanios
'We Buy the Best, We Sell
for Less' Fish Bar: all this
life and colour
suits them as they suit each other.
It is the end of April,

the season of weddings and rain.
Joe in Joe's Fags and Mags
talks about nothing all week

but Arsenal and Patrick
over the Sun and chocolate eggs
while old ladies and gentlemen

wait outside the corner shop
for Anna, leaning together
in arches of hot gossip.

It is almost summer. The weather
suits them as they suit each other.

Already the evenings are warmer.
In the small hours there is rain

and blackbirds blink awake and sing,
in love with the sound of water.

Snapshot of an Egotist

I'm the one with seven forks,
wisped hair, the bingo grin.

Behind me is a mass of knees,
fat and bone leant together

in a gloom of monotone.
I'm propped against trunks

like Brunel posed with giant chains
or Hemingway, leaning on tusks;

at ease. Hands loom, out of focus,
big as birds, but at my service.
I'm the one with all the forks.
I'm the one. There are voices

touching overhead,
talking and talking back,
senseless as the sound of rain.
This is what the grin says:

'I've got the forks. I've got the knees.
And that's enough. There's nothing else.'
Shutters click and when I laugh,
lilac blossom pops like popcorn.

Is this all my fault, or is
all this for me? I can't believe my luck.
I'm going to scream again.
This is the life. Give us a kiss.

Self-Portraits by Children

This is called Kevin.
It has two keels and two strings.
The head is hairless and fits on
like this. The torso is made of things
which smile. Not like Jack

in profile, Jack full-frontal.
The line pocked where the crayon broke.
In this mirror no one would smile
at no one. His tongue is a joke
drawn and drawn again and then crossed-out.

Jane has nine segments and a head
haired upwards like a coconut.
Clark has amoebic legs and Margaret
is a map of Trinidad—

the smell of crayon, the mirror propped
up on a table, and the thought:
this is my face or could be that. And this
is where my thinking goes. I choose
how many teeth and if I stare—

the hands aching and the face on paper
not going how the hands want it.
Already gone and done, and the mirror
flat and obvious compared with Amber

who has seven sunflowers
instead of hands, or John-Luke
crumpled up without a face. Or Kate,

who is almost nothing,
a trajectory of ink.
Just something going somewhere.

Saturday Night Fever

Working the clubface
she is flash as fish skin

> she is teeth bared and head down
> deep in the limelights

and then outside, her winter coat
begins to smell of rain
suddenly, as if the sense
has been waiting there, quietly. The streets

> go on ahead of her, net curtains
> faded to the watermark
> of yesterday's light.

She could watch them for hours,
the rows of window ornaments
which lie like advertisements
for the rictus of porcelain,

for airless evenings and nights
inside her watchful family. The knives
of silences,   the little knives
of secrets hidden and sought out.

The hide-and-seek, ready or not. *Forty-eight,*
forty-nine, a hundred. Sloughs of butterflies
trapped without understanding
in the summer house's oven.
She hides among them as she waits

to be found out. Fingers their dust,
white and allergic to the light.

Their wings are thin
as Christmas glass.
She makes her face up with their dead pollen.

Down Camden Road at midnight,
a mother's voice calling to church,

        and the breath of the girl.
        Running, running.

A Night in the Room of the Clown

All night, the smell of greasepaint
rises from a circus-ring of rugs,
the leg of a sheepskin laid out
on the creased hand of a leopardskin.

I am waiting to sleep
on the chair, at the desk
with its one drawer missing like a tooth.
Alone in the room with my shoes on.
Tented with light
from a window of street
I go through papers, looking for facts.

Like a taxman. Here's a shot
of The Great Geronimo
lookout-poised at London Zoo.
Face washed white, except
for the pelt-holes
of his small eyes and big mouth.

I pick up jokes, put them back:
juggling balls. Rubber milk
and a cut-throat, smiling out
clean from its iron backbone.

There is the ordinary sound
of voices, calling voices home
outside, and a cement truck's groan
at a rabbit's skull,
the leer of its nudity
on the headlit windowsill.

If I click on the light, skins and bones
grin at the captive audience
of themselves. I sit alone,
laughing until it hurts
at the joke of growing thin,
the tick of the clock and the clapping of rain.

Excerpts from a London Zoo Guide Book, 1928

The Zoological Gardens
are most conveniently reached
by taxi. Bears like carrots
and especially anything sweet
such as honey, golden syrup
or sweetened, condensed milk.
Learning the animals' names will make them

attentive. Keep hold of possessions.
Avoid the bear-pit when it rains.
The dark-room is in the charge of the keeper
of the Wolves' Den, and a coati is amusing
if given scent
on a small wisp
of cotton-wool.

Just here is the Aquarium
with its elaborate system of water
held in suspended reservoirs.
The tanks are lighted while the corridors are dark.

The white cobra is probably unique.
The building by the aviary
was erected for a 'sacred' white elephant
and its attendants. Most of them will beg
for food and some sit up
in very amusing attitudes.

Note the cage with radiant heat
where the lowest mammals may be seen,
the creatures which are fed at dusk,
anteaters and agoutis.

We have now reached the extreme
where tunnels and canal-bridges
lead out. Underground Railways
run on into the evening;
See Maskelyne's Mysteries
(cf.), the Music Halls and Cabarets.

The Island of Pumpkins

In the hills of the Island of Pumpkins
I go walking.
The sun burns
my white skin. I am carrying

mixed currencies. A business card.
A bag of cold blood-oranges
bought cheap on the mainland.

Here
it is the seventh week of drought
since the end of the season of rain.

Around my feet are pumpkin vines
making yokes and watchsprings,
   searching for water
        in the yellow dust.

It has taken all night to get here,
and that with good transport
and now there's nothing left to see
but the easternmost hills
of an easternmost island,

their green bowls cupped
against green bowls

and a tractor leant sideways,
catching the sun
in its broken glasshouse.

Sound is slow to come this far,
carried and dropped and then picked back
up over the fields of pumpkins—
laughter, a joke. A foreign language
with no words for *miss*.
I miss

a tongue where I am not run dry.
Here I am surface-muck.
I miss place-names familiar as salt
and the dialect of rush-hours—

a klaxon hoots
         drawn out
from the docks. There is the clank

of men unloading greenhouse glass
and blocks of ice in plastic green
as pumpkin skin wiped damp and clean—
and what I see is what I miss;

watching late trains cross
the bridge, the river. Years of rain
fallen down into the Thames.
Night falling on the homes and the homeless.

Dowsing with Whalebones

I am a follower of water.
If I stand at this junction of roads

I can divine its sound,
the bell and dirge of water

underground. The level, bubbled skin
and always the one direction.

I arrived here with the night train,
the smell of its engines and dust

a foreign language. This is the city
of dry cisterns. People sip

small measures in the bars, and grin
at intelligences of rain,
the force of it cracking their lips.

There is hopelessness in dry directions.
I get lost between the Street of the Flies

and the Street of Five Stations.
Left and right are inside of me,
compass-points are not—hopeless!

When I turn in the Square of Pigeons
my left eye is still my left eye
which was my north,
and is my south.

But these are my whalebones,
light and supple as the seethe of plankton.
I follow them to troughs and gutters
and square miles of sewer pipes

because each city has its heart
and every heart is water. Here

is the gourd-thump of an empty butt,
here is the tock of grit in wells and sumps.

Down at the end of terraces
I find the source. The tide is out

and the light flat as mud.

I sit by the embankment
on the warm stone, and take the air,

having all that I came here for:
a souvenir of pigeon feathers
the colour of magnet

and the way home, which is straightforward
as downpour,

and a bed for the night,
sweet in the morning
with the smell of the river.

A Page of a Guide to a Small Island

The island cisterns have been dry
since the war. Eat moist fruits

and walk in shade. Buy currency
in small amounts.
The cost of living is not high.

Watch out for false surcharges,
the price of meat out of season
and the slight oracles
of a thumb's imprint in Roman pottery,
    of a moth's wings
        marked with road maps
            and old sea lanes

Go walking through the old town,
where the stepped streets
smell of the thighs of pigs
and rotting cryptomeria—
but sunstroke can be dangerous.
Look out for warning signs:
burnt skin, slight dizziness, small voices,
        the guttural vowel of water,

        the struck stone
of a bat's tongue,
gauging distances.

There are new hotels each season,
more pleasure boats, less secrecy.

But do not underestimate
the strength of myth in an island state;

what has been lost was never strong—
the cracked urns
where bees hived, the muttering
and comb moulded
to one round lip. And
some things must be lost, while some things

stay for good. Sea caves hung
with looms of stone,
unfinished works of amethyst,

or the navigator's middle daughter,
waves slopped open beside her,
threading the hips of a bee.

Knotting it tight. It groans and turns
above her laughter.
Later, she'll take its wings away
and watch it roll in the summer dust
like the pigs.
Like an animal.

A Crossroads

1 WALKING IN JULY

I leave with no reason except to walk,
under the road trees, which are still and black

as wet concrete. Turn left and left and right.
This street is smoothed out new and flat

with curds and slatherings of tar,
hot through my shoes. This suntrapped square

has no name on the map. Two car alarms
panic together over rented rooms.

This is a place never meant for A–Zs or visitors:
lost space. No Dogs No Ballgames Squares

where no one hears the trees
fall and rise in their own branches.

Down here there is the sound of talk
in eyehole doorways and carpeted halls,
enquiries to help
with Missing Persons, Lost and Found.

There is the smoker's cough of police lines,
and echoed down between the flats
of Ratcliff, Ruthven, Ravenscar,
Martha's Soft Ice
Mind the Children
plays the ice-cream song.

Cold names. Officers come and go,
searching for joyriders, blip boys,
lift surfers. Pensioners shaking
their heads, shaking. 'I don't know him.'
'Not him. I have trouble with names.'
Grey skin on them, as warm and grey
as the hearts of artichokes.

As sweet as that. *Names trouble me.*
One hand moves on the public clock, or
all the hands move on all the clocks,

out through mapped streets and postal codes
and if I stand just here, just right

and look up, I can see the rain
coming, and light on aeroplanes
high and nameless, crossing time zones.

2 LAST TRAIN, NOVEMBER 1ST

Out to the bedroom-towns with their
lurch of headlights over sleeping policemen

goes the twelve-ten with half-empty seats
smelling of cigarettes and factories.

This is the dark between stations where
nobody talks to no one, and the river

looms like a high-rise
under piers and viaducts.

In the night train's public places
we are the photofit faces

watching closing-times and derelicts
out of windows puzzled with rain.

In transit nothing counts. It makes us
full of possibilities:

some of us dream of rush-hours,
some of us will be dangerous.
This is what we come to when

the overtime is gone and there is
nothing left to do but listen
for public announcements or aggression—

the voice into a cordless phone
that lies like a dentist to its loved one,

the movement of air
in tunnels and wires,

the track, which says
I am correct—
I am the click of binary
in satellite and sea-bed lines,

I am the atom in the clock,
I am the metric length of gold.
It could be you. It could be you. It could
—and from the yards outside,

gently, the hush of a city and a river,
and the smell of rain coming in
through open doors at platforms and destinations.

3 Shore Leave in Winter

Waiting for thaw in a thin country
there is small-talk and small questions.

Why here. Where from. He always tells them
how he never learned to read.
It sounds like truth and is

part truth. There were other ways to own
the shape of the road-sign of his first town.

One letter was crossed like fingers.
He copies it out on the glass of his pint.
The last letter was crossed like a heart,

a printer's symbol of the heart,
its four-valved crossroad.
That was the word

for what was always promised,
home, spelt out black on white

like the brunt sea
under spilt foam.
The last sign out by the McClean farm.

There have been other ways
to read, without the thick silt
of last names and signatures.
The hatchworked script
of ice on a ship's glass,

meaning *North*, the mouthings of trawled tons
of scad and skate. The trick of reading stars

through clouds,
the lucidity of air
over distant water

and then the water,
which accepts any writing
like paper, only disturbed by tides.

But for now there is only lights out,
shut doors, the chuff of feet,
his feet, and the cold of the rain
falling down over Warren Street.

4 Spring on the Underground

After the alarm,
she lies back in her cold spring room
taking little sips of sleep
while sunlight spills across the floor.

Inside her was a dream
of rain lessening
in a dry country.
Pines smouldered and

needles shone, dark as pepperskins.
There was the pain of being touched
and the pain of almost being touched
in a locked room, in a locked room.

Now there is the northern city
of plane trees and mackerel skies.
The sun is in;
it looks like rain. Inside the Underground

is writing she can't understand.
LOVE IS GOØD. YIDS GO HOME.
SKREWDRIVER RULES. *The alien*

should tear along the perforated strip.
She waits in offices
with her left hand warm in her right hand.
Her ticket is shaped like a tooth.

There are forms to be understood,
words to be learned: *regime. Torture.
Period of stay.* She waits. Looks out:

small children are waving
through glass at their mother
who waits without seeing.
The bows in their hair
are shaped like kisses,
small kisses placed on foreheads.
She understands something of this.

She wishes for water's amnesia,
its magic hoops and puzzle-rings
vanishing over stones
and the impressions of rain.

Her ticket number's next. She stands,
looks out again. The roads are gone
into grey downpour.

She envies that deliverance.

The Sound of Cages

We walk each other home
eating takeaway food.

Licking the guttered mustard
from the warm bones
of wrists and hands. The lit

plinths of Docklands
are behind us, and across the park
comes the sound of zoo cages,

the crash of big animals
moving against small walls.
Cages leave nothing except time
to think, and nothing else to think

except that all cages have holes.
At nights, two escaped eagle owls
hunt our tenemented blocks

from the grey cupolas of St Paul's
to the falafel stalls of Camden.

Tall as children,
their cries bring me awake

without understanding. I listen
with my eyes open.

There is the sound of fire engines
across postcodes, and sometimes
soft voices at corners,
quiet as an ambush, and sometimes

a whistling in the dark,
cold and at ease in the stone
streets. Whistling home
with meat, and without quarantine.

The Pilot in Winter

(In a remote coastal town to the south-west of Corinth is the gravesite of Norman Mackay. In accordance with Greek Christian Orthodoxy, his bones have been dug up, washed with wine, and laid in a box the length of his thigh-bone. The townspeople believe Mackay dropped the atom bomb on Hiroshima from the B29 'Enola Gay' on the morning of August 6th, 1945. There is no record of a Norman Mackay on flight-crew logs for that exercise. The population of the coastal town in winter is 300).

I

Salt fruit on a white plate.
Yorgos the waiter takes and eats
handfuls of green olives. Spits out
the stones. Outside is the noon sun
and all the young waitresses.
He watches as they hang
octopus on coat hangers;

stretched-out stars, and pink
as knickers on a washing line
and at the crusted ventilation slit
Yorgos smiles at the thought
with his eyes. It is clear weather
today, and the coast road
shimmers with its smell
of hot tar and last winter's rain

and in a while the melon man
will drive in past the old town,
on the new road,
with his cargo of green skin.

So Yorgos waits for him
and while he waits he cleans his hands
washes his forearms knuckle-white.

Opens the window. Leans out,
looking uphill to the old town
where the Pilot is, and the blood relations
in good boxes, washed in wine.

His hands smell of their bone.
He dries the skin and nails. Goes back out
into the hot light,
feeling for coins in his pocket,
shouting a price to the melon man.

II

I walk to the hills where the old town is,
and the old church with its twelve framed
Elijahs. Wheels and chariots of fire
leaved with bright tin and sweet dust.

Outside is the industry of bees
and the clink of goats. Hills away.
Sound carries easily up here

in the summer, when there is no rain
and the bone-shed door
natters when the bolt is drawn
from the outside, and I go in.

This is a dry place to come,
but cool. The air soured by wine
and the ground darkened with oil
around the doorway's light.

Here are the town's blood relatives,
who have all met,
who can be singled out
by snapshots on boxwood,
and the measurements of thigh-bone;
great-grandparents stacked up like olive crates.

The pilot's bones are stained with earth
to the colour of earth, and the skull
is turned back into the plough
of leg and rib. No lock, only
the shift of little bones
in the box as the lid is shut.

MAKI NOPMAN in chalky script.
Here there is nothing else, except
box, name and bones, and the sound
of trees shambling in the wind
from here to Corinth. Lines of high ground

silver and black with saltless fruit
over dead towns and city-states
and bloody stories, and blood guilts.
I bolt the door shut. A truck groans
down on the coastal road,

changing gears, miles away.
Overhead, fighter planes
catch the light turning inland.

III

Under the tin roof he listens
to the seven months of winter rain.

His head hurts with listening
in the dark of his room
which is white in summer
but blue in winter
with damp and shadow

and because the rain
has fallen for so long
he can smell nothing,

as if the hills with their dust
goat-shit and balsam
and the rock-shore with its rind of salt

have gone. As if he is gouged out.
He dreams of drowning
with eyes open
under the white cages of rain.
6 a.m. By the coastal road,
the pilot stands outside the bars

and under the clock-drip of trees,
telling his stories. The bomb

warm in the south-sea island sun.
Light on the city of canals,
Hiroshima, and the bomb-cloud
rising behind them like a blackout—

—all of his bloody secrets
and his bloody lies. It does him good,
the talk. He puts his head back to taste
rain through the tamarisks,

sour and clean. The petrol-station
is open, and the workers' bar.
The rest is shut. He wipes his mouth,
feeling for words, and goes inside.

Nightlight

Under the nightlight
the page is yellowing
with the clock tick,
turning back
to the colour of wood.

There is nothing to do with it
except to write
and if the writing is about nothing

then it is about nothing.
My mind is still sluiced clean
with the joy of it,
sluiced cold and clean.

Where am I in this? Right here,
lodged in the lungs and bones
of line and line.
Haven't you seen me yet?

I'm right here, touching it.
Against the paper's flat
my hand becomes
the wing of a bat
in the nightlight

the foreleg of a horse,
or what you want. The mole's claw.
Darker. The blood and knuckle-crack

of thought; the arch of fingers
amazed and quiet

pulling the pen
into its last curve.

Nocturne in Chrome &
Sunset Yellow (2006)

to HD

'*To paint the sea really well, you need to look at it every hour of every day in the same place so that you can understand its ways in that particular spot.*' —CLAUDE MONET

'*Cities give us collision.*' —R. W. EMERSON

From the Diaries of Henry Morgan, Summer 1653

And so on May Day's eve I came to London,
with John Twentyman still riding beside me,
still chastising London even as we entered her,
her great steeples rising northwards and everywhere
bells, like those of towns in certain stories,
arisen from the sea on just such nights as these.

A dour and good man John Twentyman seemed,
and prudish in all he said, remarking
that the country life is much to be preferred,
there being Works of God there, and herein
nothing that has not been touched
into its present form by the hands of men;
but I have heard poor word of him since then,
and think the less of him for his hypocrisies.

As to myself, I have since had
much joy of London. My nights have been
as nights spent in the company of lovers.
I have played merry and yet have made
much good of myself. I am eighteen,
and have chattels and lace enough
by which a stranger might judge me a fine man.
I have a brace of snaphaunce from Tourner's,
and a sword all out of Damascene.

I do not think I will go home again.
God willing, I will make my home
hie to me as it were a good mare
coming up to the Bishop's Gate
and shaking her white head
at all the bells and carillons of London.

Repossession

The first we heard of it was the silence.
There was a morning with seagulls in it.
The air was grey, and held the smell of salt,
and when the rain began at last, at noon,

a black van pulled in by the off-licence,
so silently you had to look, and out
got the bailiffs . . . unassuming men, not
well-built as you might expect, or even

wide in the shoulders. They went to the house
with the flying buttresses where the road
gives out at the end onto railway land,
and took the door right off its hinges, one

talking down to the other in a voice
so gentle it might never have been used
to speak of violence. Which is what they did,
the smaller of them each time carrying

the chattels out, while the tall one appraised
the estimated value of the bed,
the clothes-wringer, the clothes, even some seeds
the people there had meant to plant that Spring.

They frogmarched metal shutters from the van
and bolted down the door and the windows.
Then they were done, and the van was pulling
away into the rain, which smelled of tides,

the rime blown thirty miles from Southend,
and the couple who lived in that last house
came home, the woman first, trying her hand
at kicking down doors, the man returning

later, one or the other coming round
for the loan of a crowbar. Her hands bled
before they left. We saw them again once,
by chance, the two of them sat next to us

in traffic East of Clapton. None of us
had the time to wave, and neither of them
really seemed to see us there, their faces
turning just then to look at something else.

An accident, perhaps. This isn't what
I meant to talk to you about.
The thing is this.

After the repossession men had gone
the place went up for auction, but no one
offered a price. The bank was stuck with it.
And years went by, in which the house became

homeless. The garden sank down in a tide
of lost property. Shopping trolleys stacked
with shopping bags and shopping magazines
and bottles full of groundwater and mould

suspended like marvels of medicine
and earth accumulated by the rain.
The bushes garlanded with two-for-one
takeaway menus, tin cans, foam cups, string,

the straight-backed chair where foxes sat enthroned,
the mattress where an old man slept all Spring,
the kitchen sink full of the earthenware
of mushrooms and cracked blocks of ThermoLite
dumped there, as if someone once meant to build
on those foundations of abandonment.

All this was years ago. And now you're here,
the two of you scything the bittersweet,
hopeful and very young, pulling up weeds,
weeding discarded shirts and shoes and skirts,

cutting the brambles off above the roots
so that you'll see them back before too long,
but here you are all the same, both of you
young enough not to give up for the want

of trying. And you've come at the right time,
in Spring. Already the garden you've cleared
is taking in the air, the taste of salt
the wind brings thirty miles from the sea.

Soon crocuses will break up to the light,
yellow as eggs cracked clean into a glass,
and flowers that you never knew were there
or never knew were real will appear

out of the yard the bank once tried to own,
and finding themselves nothing else to wear,
will put on buds that open to the air
like mouths containing promises, like hands

containing gifts, like small fists opening
in gestures that say *Here*, and which say *Here*.

To a Boy on the Underground

The laptop cauls your face with light,
unflattering and glutinous.
The iPod plugs your ears with ambient noise.
If you would only disconnect

you'd see the Underground's dark tract
unearthed. The tube train coiling out
into sharp shadows, sunlight cutting in
between ramrod Victorian blocks,

and the sous-chef or waiter who basks
in the sun in a restaurant backyard,
and the underwriters, auditors or clerks
who lean out of high windows like the girls

in folklore, one dangling a cigarette,
one seeming to be savouring the smells
of pizza ovens, Peking duck and piss,
the air half-edible and wholly foul,

and here and there green hanging gardens,
sunken gardens, roof gardens,
yards like cesspits, and everywhere carnivals
of people, the crowds embracing their collision.
Only disconnect, and all this will be yours, my son.

A Year in London

JANUARY

A Free Advertisement for Kabul John's Café, Kilburn Market

You're late, you're late, you're late the blackbird says,
and true enough the starlings are settling,
jostling and scuffling the snow from the trees,
imitating console games and children's cries
and mobile phones and traffic lights and what might be
the trajectory of an unidentified flying object,

and night is closing in so fast,
the day so ahead of itself
that those in search of some last purchase
go lolloping through the snow,
clopping and crumping through the fresh white fall
into the fish-grey slush between the market pitches,

and the stalls are all packing up for the night,
the man at Max Classic Trade Price Shoes
and the woman at Wanshika's Quality Underwear
who might be Wanshika in the flesh
putting away their luxury goods,
leaving nothing behind that isn't
firmly nailed to the pavement.

The lights under the covered walks
are switched off one by one, until
only Kabul John's Café is lit,
its neon spanning out into the street,

the smell of All Day English Breakfast Specials
expanding in the January air
as thick as lard. So warm and nourishing
that passers-by with nowhere left to go
stop in their tracks, breathe its emollient,

open the foggy sheet glass door,
stamp the mire from their boots,
sigh out the cold, and bow, and enter in.

FEBRUARY

Hungover, and forgetting to bring water,
I lean by the Leg of Mutton Pond
and watch the dogs that come to drink.

The tallest go in like horses,
slake their thirsts, and stagger out
skeletonized, glabrous, and still proud.

They mean no harm to anyone,
and warm the earth by virtue of their shit.
Under the oaks by West Heath Road
the soil is fertile and sweet
and loathsome as mechanically recovered meat.

Nothing will express its gratitude
today, but in the next week or the next,
snowdrops will thaw into the nourishment.

The corms of winter aconites
will go off like long-buried ordnance,
the English lawns will lock their roots
into trace elements of blood and bone,
the little shreds of life that are the birds
will expurgate the soil in their hunger,

and the first crocus that grows there
will unfurl its vermilion innards,
unsheathe its tenuous head,
and finding goodness in the world—
and much not good, but to its liking—
will satisfy its own thirst on the rich, bright air.

March

Up at 4 a.m. to piss,
you are surprised by yesterday's rain
still tapping at the skylight to be let in.

Such patience. No friend of ours
invited for an evening
would wait so long for either of us.

You are still skinned with sleep as warm as milk,
so that you say to the rain, *I'm not dressed yet,*

and hear the wind in the chimney-breast
answer, *I own this ground and will again,*
in one gust, and in the next,
Nothing is for nothing.

You see the kitchen table has been laid
with a clean slate of moonlight,
and the bills we've not yet paid
for the winter months of North Sea gas
have been arranged like place settings.

At night, this house is not ours to own,
and something else receives its visitors.
A helicopter overhead goes
ploughing through the force which drives the rain,
the chopper moving closer, house to house
along the empty course of Watling Street
as if it too has been invited.

And the rain at the threshold still says nothing,
but taps and taps to be let in,
and the wind lodged in the chimney shrieks,
I own this acreage,
and will again. Nothing is for nothing.

April

The first chess players have returned,
seven old men in shy grey tweeds
outside L'Algeroise Café,
their hands among the pawns, hungry as birds
eating a field bare of seed in Spring.

One is resolving problems from *The Times*,
one sips a tulip-glass of Turkish tea,
one licks his lips and risks his queen to check,
one chain-smokes with the sun warm on his back.

One talks incessantly, remembering games
in Budapest and Oran and Marseilles.
One eats small almond pastries from L'Algeroise,
his sweet fingers congealing to the pieces.
The last sits with a child on his knee
and plays with her as if she is a game
he has no talent for, but means to learn.

Cars head past like a river tide in Spring.
The grocer's boy from the Food & Wine
spills pears and avocados in the gutter
and goes down on his knees to rescue them.
Old women with high colour in their cheeks
buy leavened bread and withered aubergines.
The hoarding on the Bon Pain Bakery
changes from Ford to Marlboro to Lynx
to Chanel Number 5 and back again,

and by L'Algeroise, only the child
looks up from the rooks and sees that Spring
is drawing in beside her like a train,
all belch and brass and noise; that Spring
is just arriving all around her,

the look on her face going up and away,
over the old men at their games,
over the boy who is rescuing pears,
over the hoardings and aubergines,
up like a kite she goes into the Spring.

May

The street outside jointed with leery boys
and girls dressed up as sweethearts for the night
and buntings of blood draped in the gutters
where half the bouncers weigh into a fight,

or worse, weigh up the odds and make themselves
scarce as needs be when one needs must to piss.
Like two fat ladies from the bingo hall
next door, they shake their heads at all the mess:

like sumo wrestlers bored of slender wives
they look hungry for more, all petulance
and disappointment with the muck and maul
spilling across the street, as if they'd hoped

for better things tonight. For more than this,
the girls down on their knees, missing their shoes
in all the fuss. And still there are the queues
of punters loving it, waiting their turns

to push inside, into the sallow gloom
where the ticket woman and the cloakroom man
wait for their offerings of coats and coins
before they'll let a single soul pass through

into the wash of glitterball-spun light,
onto the dance floor, where the air is warm
and everyone is diamonded with stars,
where anyone can star in their own film,
a musical where star-crossed lovers meet
and dance, and slow-dance underneath the stars
until the stars themselves blush and wink out.

And though sequels are never half as good,
they're all the night's dancers will think about
as they walk out into the May-damp streets
alone or arm-in-arm, wrapped in their coats

or lacking even those. And Cricklewood
colder and darker than it was before,
the takeaways full of forlorn lovers
all much the worse themselves for wear and drink,

waving at taxis that slip past the lights
to Hampstead, where clients tip ten percent,
and not their guts, and don't try and get out
as soon as they see somewhere else they like,

and now there is no going back.
Ashtons is gone. The hall has been knocked down,
the land sold on. Pigeons sit
in rows along the hoardings, like
those boys who never brought themselves to dance
but stood all night and necked their beers:

Ashtons has closed for good,
and almost any night will find me glad,
loving the quiet as I work,
as I work now, or make us food, or wait
for my own love to come home through the dark,

and only once, walking home
from some night better never spent,
it seemed to me that the Broadway missed
something. A quality of brightness,
as if the lights had gone out all at once
across the neighbourhood,

and I thought of this and that.
Mostly the girls, who were pretty sometimes,
and always seemed to be looking for things
they'd either not yet found, or left behind
somewhere else. Their best friends and best earrings,

their drinks and shoes and coats and darling boys,
and dreams and last dances and happy endings.

JUNE

*But Cricklewood is mine. I discovered it. No one will go there again.
It is like the sunken town in the fairy story that rose just every May
Day eve and lived for an hour and only one man saw it.*

—T. S. Eliot, 1911

    Someone in that house must be in love
    with scented geraniums:
    there are so many of them,
    all bunched and grubby and alive
    out in the whitewashed yard.

    I thought it was the younger
    of the old tight-lipped black-eyed women
    both of whom now and then
    slouches out onto the steps,
    squats down by the slipshod pots,
    and leans up to the baskets
    on tiptoes in green-furred slippers
    with a long-necked green watering can.

    But neither of them ever seems
    to take much pleasure in the task,
    and after all, it could be the men
    who find loveliness in that garden,

one of the Serbs or the Bosnian,
or the Corfiot who always looks
down at heel but in good spirits,
or the shy Somali in the eastern-facing room
who lives his days out in night-shifts,
any of those who come to live
here, of all places.

After all, why not them?
They are all single men, and prone to love.
On warmer evenings they come outside
to sit in the boarding house yard
and play at backgammon, or read
second-hand paperbacks
in their several alphabets.

Once, with a fence needing repair
we went there looking for labour.
The windowsills were stacked
with working mens' shoes
and cartons of milk.
The hallway was unlit and sour
with the odour of linoleum,

and the man who took the work
came early the next day,
refused the food we offered,
ate his own, and worked
until the light was gone outside,

carpentering the lengths of wood
with skill and patience and no word
of English but one for a greeting
and one more for thanks in the evening.

Afterwards we recognised him,
one man in several, walking home
along the dark blocks of the high road,
past the derelicts sat propped
in the doorways of derelicts,

none of them with a lift in their step,
each of them trudging home,
but somehow trudging home,
back to their accommodations,
the one room, the timed strip
of light above the washbasin:

back through the broken concrete
of the yard, the flowers thriving there
leaving a scent on each man's skin,
something for them to remember,

something to bring them back in years to come
here, to Cricklewood,
as if this was a time and place they ever loved.

July

At the Wing Yip Chinese Supermarket

The old fishmonger with the cropped grey hair
leaves to her young apprentices the tasks
she has no appetite left for,
and no longer takes pleasure from.

Her eyes slide over heaps of grey croaker
and customers she doesn't know by name,
though no one lifts the lobsters from their tanks
or fillets dog-shark except her:

to her go all the finer works.
She guts the yellowtail and gilt-head bream,
the scales adhering to her braced forearm
until it seems transmogrified,

her skin shining, sequinned, and slicked with blood.
She beheads char, cuts through the spines
of congers, rinses viscera and bones
from her raw red knuckled fingers,

and goes out to the locked ice-room,
coming back in with sabrefish
unsheathed over her shoulder blades,
the cold escaping in a wash

of fog around her boots and jeans.
She looks in the eyes of the wealthy men
who buy such things, and nods, and says,

Yes, fresh.
The eyes of the great greyhoundish heads
laid meekly in her scaled hands
as cold and bright as jewels, or pommel stones.

August

when pigeons like *dei ex machina*
descend improbably out of the air

wobble like airships skimming through the tops
of trees which sink under their tea-pink weights

until each grandee bungee-jumps or belly flops
downwards in great soap-operatic terrifying swoops

into the sweet dark shining feather-bedness of the fruits

September

And sometimes months go by when London
leaves me cold, hating the starlessness
of its illuminated midnights
and the muck of noise on the Edgware Road
where a glut of goods is bought and sold
24–7. I lose my appetites,
wanting for nothing for so long
that I dream of nothing worth wanting,
not the pearskin lacquer furniture
stacked on the pavements, or the duckbone jade
the old men wear to fortify their hearts,
or the bagels trawled from boiling vats,
the lobsters knuckled down in blue-lit tanks,
or the girl in the summer dress who eats
priceless white peaches with the juice
running down her wrists like pale sinews,
or the basements impregnated with the smells
of tamarinds and naan and cooking wine,
or the people in the road outside
who seem to move in the way that starlings
hinge themselves together in the sky.

Then something will happen to make me remember
what it is I love here,
what I am wanting for. It will be some grey September.
I will look outside.

In the garden
the goldfish are nuzzling
at heaps of soft late summer rain.

If I could have only one thing,
it would be some moment like this,
when one small fact puts all the facts right,

when the rain clears the London air
and my thoughts lie suddenly clean
and bright in the strength of their own wellspring.

October

October, and you buy pomegranates,
the Sabian grocer on Shoot Up Hill
putting one extra in the bag for you
because he insists it matches your hair,

which I had always thought was only brown,
chestnut at most, like the nuggets of seeds
the trees in Gladstone Park are letting fall,
as if I'd never looked at you at all.

I will never have seen enough of you.

NOVEMBER

London—there's a rhythm to the name,
its ending an echo of its beginning,
as if *London* were the name for somewhere
full to the brim with its own echoes.

I think of the sound of ordnance
each November, the guns echoing
through the fog and the minute's silence
in remembrance of themselves,

and the bomb's echo that shook the air
miles north of the NatWest Tower
the night my father came cycling home,
shepherding the bike into the hall
before he said he wasn't feeling well,
his heart foundering in our hands,

and the sound of fireworks, that night
we stopped on the stairs in Bell Wharf Lane
to watch them fall across the river,

the thunderous openings like hands, or
arms thrown wide in embraces,
each one falling short of our places
on the black steps of the wharf-side stairs.

Those rockets coming down in glorious gold
into the river. Who were they for?
How would we ever know? The echoes
filling up the streets around us
with a sound like *London*, a sound like *Lon*

Don. And all that brilliance was ours
in our dreams that night, even
if none of it was ever meant for us.

DECEMBER

What frost there was is nearly gone by the time I'm up to look for it. I take a book I'm meant to read and go up the hill to Gladstone Park. The Pleasure Grounds are still unlocked. The air is pricked with awns of ice that settle in my two-week beard. A man on the bench by the ginkgo tree hunkers down against the cold. He cups his cigarettes against the frost, smokes each one to the end and drops the ends between his feet. He tips the ash from a fifth before he crushes it out under his foot. He waits for the last to cool before he picks them up, one by one, and puts them back in the golden packet. He takes it with him when he goes.

I walk home past the pumping station. One day they'll sell it off for flats. Inside its nave, the reservoir casts slatted ripples up the walls. They say ice is lighter than water. As a child I thought it hung above the ponds on the Heath like the vaults of churches. At the Irish butcher's I buy what I can for the change in my pocket. Indoors, I cut the meat, slide it along the knife and board, into the pot of leftovers, letting it warm over the flame. Outside the snow begins. The light on the phone has lit itself. I leave it and take off my coat. I go upstairs in the dark, holding onto my thoughts. Balancing them, one ripple against the other, as if I were carrying water.

TV Dinner

You at the counter, cutting onions into moons,
one hand aloft to heel away the tears,

me watching ants on the television,
two of them, drinking a bridal cup
of rain, holding the drop between them,
the bright waterskin unbroken.

The clock by the window striking nine,
the pendulum drowsing,
the ants drinking from their upheld moon,

and you coming to stand beside me,
your hand coming to rest on me,
your eyes on the television,
and your face all wet and salt from weeping.

Synthesis

Cutting into colour,
wormcasts and turds of cadmium,

chiselling the new violet,
squibs and swabs of cobalt blue,

drilling one iota of lead white
into an ammonite of best vermilion,

Matisse feels as if he is
a sculptor carving into stone.

Somewhere, he once came across
a line of Pliny, old and sour,
bristling at younger pleasures,

*Now India contributes the ooze of her rivers
and the blood of dragons and of elephants—*
his picked bone being Rome's painters
dipping their wicks in shameless eastern taints.

It is summer, and every year
he still comes back to Paris
having wintered in Nice,
though there's no peace here for anyone.
It is a congeries of passers-by
and motorcars and early callers,

the synthesis of light and noise
unnatural as the latest pigments
sold for a packet at Sennelier's,
the brightest new ultramarine,
or the brown mummy, which is composed
of no embalmed flesh, the Egyptians
having brought that trade to an end.

But here he is again,
back in the city in high summer,
chipping germs of pigment from the palette,

and still finding
how much he loves
the way that as dawn breaks
the sounds of the street below
fade up and penetrate into this room,

just as the arsenic in the violet
has penetrated his fingers,
turning their whorled impressions
into ten works of vivid synthesis.

Gravity

How can there have been a time when this
still lay undiscovered: light falling
through the trees, and the first leaves falling
all at once into the cold evening,
leaves through light in endless gravity?

By the church where I sang as a boy
and dreamed I'd be a scientist
I break my walk, and sit quite still.

How still must I sit to hear the dead?
Through the obduracy of the yews
the wind shuffles and stills and runs on

into the fallen leaves by the locked church door,
with the sibilance of the Lord's Prayer.

Forgive us our trespasses.
Dusk falls into the streets.

The owl quarters its territories.
Still I am not still enough.

The Gifts

Fishing the warm newspaper off his chips,
Now, where have I seen that before? he said,
and smoothed it out in the street with the wind
worrying at the parcels in our hands.

And there was nothing printed there but words.
His words, worked at, meant as the best of him,
marked up with sauce and vinegar, and scraps
and haddock shovelled in over his name.

I thought his pride was hurt, and understood
nothing then of the writer's pride he found
in coming on his words like that. Strangers
queuing for them in the shop's salt brightness,

and, block by block, nursing them through the streets
like long-awaited news. Like heartfelt gifts.

The Nightworkers

Long after midnight
the railwaymen
work in pairs along the line
surreptitiously, at first,

the track stones
under their boots
trod like ice
into ruts.

The clocks stop for them.
Nothing comes
while they mend their ways.
Nothing goes. The night trains

rest in their stables.
The mainline lies
bright as cobweb

and the voice of the first man to speak
becomes a grand thing in the darkness
and the workers who follow
lope like so many bogeymen
through the lights of the gantry towers.

We lie awake for hours.
We rise like sleepers
hauled from beds of stone.
We cannot close our ears to the North
the railwaymen bring in their laughter.

Only towards morning will a word
turn them, one by one
homewards, calling names
and names and goodbyes as they go,

and though we'll be released to sleep
we'll lie awake in those small hours
until we're sure we've heard the last
there is to hear. We'll hang on their words,

listening for the lightness in them,
the lift in their voices at first light,
the eagerness they have in going home,
and even for the way they seem
to wake from sleep or dreams themselves,

as if they've slept their lives away, and now
find themselves boys again, waking in winter
to yell their names clear across miles of snow.

The Orator

'The people of Amathus, in revenge for his having laid siege to their town, severed the head from the dead body of Onesilus and hung it up above their gates. In time it became hollow, and was occupied by a swarm of bees, who filled it with honeycomb.'

HERODOTUS, 'The Histories'

Monday finds him early at his station,
squatting on his haunches on the corner
outside Barclays Bank, eating hand-me-downs
from McDonald's, then unfolding long shanks,
pocketed hands, and a skull losing hair
as if someone in love has stroked him there
more often than the flesh of him can bear,

and so comes to a standstill, his back flat
to the thronged house of the moneylenders,
the first words already poised on his lips,
the rest of them gathering up inside,
until he lifts his bandaged megaphone
and opens up his teeth to let them out.

THOSE WHO COME TO FIND THE LORD
—Napthalis says through a plague of static—
THOSE WHO WAIT TO LOOK FOR HIM
ONLY AT THE ELEVENTH HOUR
WILL DIE AT TEN THIRTY, Napthalis says,

but the English rain has again begun
its interrupted centuries of fall
and no one stops to listen, though some
look back at him with surreptitious spite,

the man with the golden bee in his bonnet,
the figure in the knitted cap and parka
with God lodged like a dove in his mind,
and a curse on the house of each commuter:
sharp as splinters lodged in careless hands
are his offerings, his diatribes.

Not even a smile on a swan-black girl
assuages him. But the days are long,
and evenings find him murmuring
the spirituals that his aunts taught him,
the old women with ermine eyes,
tough as yardfowl, their mingled voices
sour-sweet as the juice of June plum,

and faint, so that they come to him now
only as visitations in his dreams;
Dara, with the dozen rings,
Maud, who sometimes read to him

when he was a boy in a town called Rest
in a house on the river on the green island
he hasn't seen in forty-seven years
and won't see again now before Heaven.

DO NOT HURRY INTO ETERNITY
he says with rationed fire and brimstone
to the overstanding gentleman
who stops to give him a toll of change
but should know better than to go

yarding through the rain like a madman,
sneezing all the way like a dog barking—
all teeth—to reach Iceland by closing time,

the newspaperman across the road
a balancing muezzin, when Napthalis
starts to hum again,
Isaiah a sweet venom on his tongue,
while the rain from the north stings his face,

and the sky is leaded with more to come,
or with the dark of the world that waits
to fall, Napthalis thinks, though he knows

that in Cricklewood on a Monday night
nothing is fit to bear the weight
of being anything more than it seems,

and just as Napthalis is just Napthalis,
so the darkness that surrounds him
is nothing more or less than darkness.

Amphibians

No cats out in this weather,
only the dog with its hair slicked flat
in the yard beside the timber depot,
and the fish in the blue garden urn
mouthing at the water's surface,

as if, when their gold lips break through its tension,
they'll swim out from their deep enamelled cistern
and up and up into the deep blue downpour.

The Lighthouse Keeper's Cat

In 1895 a new species of wren was discovered on St Stephen's Island off New Zealand. The Stephen's Island Wren was only ever identified from dead specimens, the last having been killed by the lighthouse keeper's cat.

All day it lies as if extinct,
coiled like an ammonite
at the foot of the spiral stairs,
or basks in the primacy of sunlight.

Only at night will it bring him gifts.
The lighthouse keeper wakes
to the watchworks of ghost crabs
left for dead, and to wrens so slight

that more than once he misses them,
and twice takes them for living things,
the fish bone teeth of the tom
having held them so carefully.

Before he came to the island
the keeper dreamed of the loneliness,
the rocks and the flotsam of the wrecks,
and found all this, but also found

the bright peoplings of birds,
the balance of hawk and gull
over green inland hills, swifts wintering,
and hummingbirds, greener than green.

He climbed the damp helix of stairs
and found the lamps on their axis
grown solid with a weld of rust,
fossilised in the wet salt air,

and nineteen days in the mending,
with only the eyes of the cat
moving around the rounded room,
the animal turning and turning about

like a warning of something happening
or yet to happen. Those first weeks
he slept not knowing yet what he had done,
not knowing that a part of him

left his side each night and went
out into the green and greener hills,
uncoiling under the lamp of the moon
to bring him back his small, delicate gifts.

Five Ways of Looking at my Grandfather

I

Here is Basil Philip's microscope,
human as the things humans possess
too deeply, loving too much
those possessions that come to possess them.

How well he cared for these six lenses,
each spare eye snug in its metal case,
each case nested in its velvet socket
like a shotgun shell cast out of brass.

The lidded cylinders have kept their shine,
the fragile concavities of glass
their strength. The measure of each gaze
is etched under the maker's sign,

and on the slides, with their salmon-fine
leaves of spinal nerve and miner's lung,
Doctor Basil Philip Hill has signed

his handiwork (his writing so small
that he might have been measuring out
valuable medicine, and not ink,

drop by blue Indian drop),
so that something of Basil Philip
survives him in his instrument,

even though nothing of him remains
on these cold surfaces; not so much
as a single fingerprint.

II

Here he is, his face pressed to the glass,
watching the blackbirds guzzling his redcurrants,

fingers leaving puzzled labyrinths
on the pantry window where he leans,

eyes (what colour were they? I recall
blue, but none of us are blue-eyed boys—)

blue eyes on the blackbirds, like a cat's,
the garden bright and still as tapestry

except for the birds, burgling the swags
of all the sweetness that he cares for,

so that he mutters at their flit and flicker,
and chews on his moustache, as if it could

nourish him, with such sweet nourishment
as birds might find on a cold morning,

and without knowing it, he grinds his teeth,
as if he means to drop the birds stone-dead,

as if he held those sweet throats in his mouth.

III

After the death of his middle son,
Basil Philip brooked no carelessness
and let the past into the future
as sparingly as he would measure
air and ether for the surgeon.

The dead were not to be seen or heard
in the house with the room where the boy had died,
but the room itself was full of nothing,
like a vacuum in a dome of glass,
and the air in that house always seemed
as botched and harmful as an overdose.

When was it that he gave up hope
of wedded love? Or was that her?
She grieved with less care for her happiness,
and many years before she died,
gave up also the ghosts of memories.

So one forgot, and one refused
to dwell on things better forgotten,
and neither chose to speak of it again.

And if they went on loving, then their love
was never seen or heard itself, as if
it wasn't something which they wished to prove
to anyone, and least of all themselves,

and if they did not, then the *not* was pushed
into a corner, like old medicine,
or hidden in the shadows of the house
like a child playing at hide-and-seek,

a boy crouched in the dusty attic dark,
listening to someone count a hundred
and wishing only never to be found.

IV

Each night, the headlights of his car
turn in late from the Royal Berkshire,
all the things that remain unsaid
there in the hall in the darkness with him,

and late at table, flushed, he asks for
carrots, mustard, sauce-boat, cruet
through the media of those who live,

comments on the cauliflower,
observations on the weather,
passed through one son or the other

as if they are concavities of glass
through which a man might know his wife
without having to catch her eyes.

He doesn't glance up when she drops her knife
but works his soup, head down, as if he eats
guest house food at a table by himself,

and so they all four eat as if alone.
Or as if, somewhere in the room, a fifth
stands like a man outside a restaurant,
drawn by the light, the foggy glass, the smell of meat,
wanting for company, or nourishment, or rest.

v

My favourite memory of him:
old and not much belittled
by the wrong-ended focus of the years,

moving a pumpkin from place to place
in the best room of a smaller house.

The fridge is full of chocolate,
great bars and cakes of it, and nothing else.
He has no one but himself to please.

He carries the fluted, green-gold weight
of the first pumpkin of the year
from the piano to the mantelpiece
to keep it in the ripening light,

as carefully as if, with his care,
all will be well in the end. As if,
with care, nothing will come to dispel

the light that settles on the windowsill
and gathers like a harvest in that room.

The Woman Who Likes Standing Under Trees in the Rain

The woman who likes standing under trees in the rain.
The woman who liked whistling like a man.
The woman who stayed a night and laughed
in her sleep. The woman who stayed a night
and who I didn't see again

for seven years, then stood there smiling
as if we'd never spent a night apart.
The woman who only liked kissing
heavy smokers. The woman who dreamt
I threw her from a moving train.
The woman who said *do what you want with me*
and wept when I did.

The woman who loved the smell of blood
and petrol stations. The woman who loathed
the smell of fireworks. The woman who hated
carnations, and never much liked music.

On journeys, stuck in traffic,
or leant to catch the small talk of a smoker,
or under the pyrotechnic flowers
of New Year's Eves and bonfires,

I catch myself thinking of them,
recalling what they did to me and me to them,
and don't wish there were more of them
half so much as I once did,

and still, will sometimes stop and try to think
what it was I ever liked or loved
about a woman who never much liked music.

Nine in the Morning in the Station Bar

What does the man in the old brown suit
say to the Old Masters on the wall
so softly that no one else can hear?

And what do the Masters say to him
that makes him flinch and turn to the room
and crow, his voice abruptly rising,

'You'll all be here till the cows come home,
bastards,' by which he means *forever*,
since no cow in a fit state of mind
would be seen dead or alive in here—

The Shire Bar, St Pancras station—
in this or any other century
(although the pub menu does offer
balti with the wording, *tender meat*).

The jukebox plays *Relax, Don't Do It*,
the TV with the sound turned down
follows the Teletubbies homewards,

and worst of all, the barman nods,
and one of the drinkers makes a face
as if to say that about trains, at least,
the old man in the suit is never wrong.

The Teletubbies rediscover shadows.
Frankie goes on and on to Hollywood.
Nine in the morning in the station bar,
and nobody comes in, and nobody goes home.

Yellow

All night she keeps the car radio on,
driving from station to station. Bhangra,
long waves, police calls, *Walking on the Moon*.
In the morning her life is behind her

and light comes shearing through the Southern rain.
She stops to take pictures of a rainbow,
the span of it above the contraflow
so still, as if nothing has yet fallen,

not her out of her life nor this downpour
through all the empty places of the sky.
Daffodils wave their yellow heads at her
and suddenly she thinks of poetry:

beautiful things. The perfect words you say
only later, too late, driving away.

A Bowl of Green Fruit

I ask for love;
she brings me breakfast kisses.
I ask my love for love
and she gives me green fruit in winter.

A bowl of green fruit.
Nothing ripe or ready.
Only the hard hearts of apples,
the acid in their whiteness,
the riddles of green oranges.

I say, I asked for love.
Why did you give me
a bowl of green fruit? She says:

wait.
And so we do,
the taste of the kisses

sweetening in our mouths,
the hearts softening,
the riddles undoing themselves.

The Wave

In the small hours, the first snow
falls and disappears and falls and

holds to itself,
the ground beneath already sprung with growth.

You bed the blunt new hyacinths in straw
and cut the last hard bud
from the damask rose you planted
last winter by the kitchen door,

and stand there with it in your hand,
out in the dead and buried yard,
as if you are asking yourself
What should I do with this?

How small my writing has become.
All day news of the dead rolls in.

We have observed the silences,
and given. What more can we give?

The death toll mounts every morning.
It grows unspeakable. You wash and dress

by the television's Morse of light,
the volume muted on the silences
which go on here and there around the world
and which, laid end to end, would render us
speechless for life. You check your purse,

keys, travelcard, and look back as you leave
in case you've left the television on,

as if the light that washes our dark room
could still come flooding out. Who would you save
if it did? And look, the flats above the shops
are all awash with that submarine light

that the news brings, and those out on the street
walk fast, as if each of them would escape
something unthinkable. This knowingness.
Nobody knows what else to do with it
but bear it, and it isn't finished yet.

There is much more that we could know,
and nobody can tell where it will stop,
or if it ever will. This is the news.
What should I do with this? you say, and then
What should I do with this?

Horse Chestnuts

Ever since summer blew their candles out
they've nursed their loss, and now their plots are hatched.

They've mined the wind. The thud of their hulls
sounds louder than our own footfalls
as we set out to walk away a night
spent poorly, in vindictive argument.

Under the avenues, the air is fogged
with the rancour and sulphur of leaf-rot,
chill after the first hard night of winter.

What's the good of talking, when our talk
brings us to this? And so we say nothing,
walking in silence under the silence
of the chestnuts, our quarrel growing
cold in the morning's greater coldness;

so, bit by bit, the day belittles us,
and with us our mistakes. Our slights seem slight
under the limbs that overshadow us
where nothing cares for us, but nothing cares
how long it takes for us to make things right.

We walk until, by silent compromise,
our hands brush past each other, and then hold.

Hold fast, my love, because there is still good
in what we have, and we will find it out.
Because there is still good for us to give,
and one to the other we will give it.

Hold tight. There's good in us, as there is
inside the sharp, green hulls of the chestnuts,
which open as we tread them underfoot,

halving to reveal themselves, not cold,
or spent, but bright as bloody, beating hearts.

Summer Late Night Opening

My god is this whole bloody place
gone to the bloody dogs tonight?
says the man in second place
behind the woman with blue hair
at checkout number five, his face
slick as the sleach in the street outside
where the roadmenders have left the road unmade.

Here is a soul who by default
moves through his days slouched like a bear,
his musculature buried under
rolls and cauls of spoiled fat
until he rears upright in anger
—as he does now—his nylon shirt
stained through with sweat from crotch to shoulder.

What's wrong with everyone tonight?
he says, and, *Is this lady mad?*
he asks, but finds he gets no answer,
because to disagree might goad him further,
and to agree would be too rude,

since, yes, the blue woman seems mad,
something in her gone haywire,
the balance of the air around her
full of the frizz and fizz and slide
of whatever thing it is that ails her.

She has now packed her shopping cart
so many times we've all lost count,
each time unpacking it again
to stare down at the things she's bought
in frank, innocent wonderment:
the eggs as smooth as eggs!
the Stagg Silverado Chicken-in-a-Can!

That's it! exclaims the ursine man,
and shambles out into the street
without the rice he meant for supper.

On the way home we see her again,
the vision of the blue woman,
standing by the green traffic lights,
gazing up with her mouth open
as if they are a visitation.

What is wrong with us tonight?
It is the first evening of June
and the crowds are out on the streets.
Everyone is coming down
like children out of school for summer.

Perhaps we are a little mad.
The air around us hums with it.
Perhaps we are all mad with hunger,
mad with everything that hunger
might conceivably be felt for.

Which is to say—mad for each other;
mad for these short nights of summer;
mad for the heat of the darkness
in which the moths above us
burn themselves up like comets
in the auras of the street lights,
in the pleasures of their madness.

Nocturne

Full moon tonight
and the snow falling,
as if the moon could shine so bright
that it would melt the snow by morning.

Chiswick Eyot
to Whistler's Mooring,
Bell Wharf Stairs to the Embankment,
Dark House Steps to the Barrier Building—

How far you've walked,
though you've been walking
this way so long you can forget
what year it is or where you're going.

This is constant:
the river's passing,
the undertow of its descent,
though all around it has been changing

every minute,
the city nothing
if not forever inconstant.
Some days you can't escape the feeling

that all is spent,
that you are running
out like the Thames into the waste
of the scoured North Sea: that there's nothing

still to be learnt,
or no more learning
that you would want to have by heart,
having no want left for anything.

Eat Your Heart Out
says the lit hoarding
up on the bridge by Parliament,
the snowflakes dancing and skimmering

as they go out,
white sparks vanishing
into the river's firmament.
This is the vein and the heart of it,

the Thames at night,
the city sleeping
under the clock tower's movement,
the slow toll of Big Ben foundering

up in the white,
and all this carving,
the generals poised in granite,
the dragon-skulls and cannon-bones

of horses rendered into stones,
the sentinels of kings and queens,
the epigraphs of the ammonites.

Are we there yet?
Something is saying
just ahead, where the dearth of light
hides anything it might be doing.

Are we there yet?
like a kid whining
by the turning, in the blind spot
you didn't mean to find this evening

or any night.
You must be leaving.
Don't look back now. Pick up your feet,
and keep walking. *And keep on walking*

Some Thoughts on Poetry

I think of the words of poetry as physical things. They have their own qualities of consistency and durability. Until they are given to an audience, words can be recast like gold into rings or teeth, or moulded like raw clay. Recorded words can never be fired ceramic-hard: they stay malleable. Like oils in painting, works of words change subtly with time.

Poetry is a shaping and carving, and the poet's methods can be lined up on the page like a sculptor's tools: rhyme, rhythm, line-breaking, repetition. These are power-tools and etching acids. Using these implements without care and control is like sandblasting a sculpture. I have always been interested in what, precisely, each of these tools does. This short essay is just me picking up a handful of tools, looking them over, putting them down. I hope it explains something about my own poetry.

What do line-breaks and verse-breaks do to language? A good break has something in common with a well-placed comma. A line break in the wrong place is like a full stop. In the middle of a sentence. But stanzas and line-breaks are more flexible than the hard ink of standard punctuation. Breaking can emphasise a word, or the space between words. It can back up a rhyme or rhythm, or it can syncopate. It can give a poem space, or its absence can create density.

Most of all, line-breaks let poetry take breath. They are as natural as breathing. They breathe in clear white paper, which becomes pan of the poem and which balances the intensity of lyrical poetic writing. They should never happen by chance. They shouldn't fit into a pattern artificially. The genius of Shakespeare's sonnets is that line breaks don't just happen every ten beats: they happen where they naturally belong.

I often use strong, driving rhythms and internal rhymes in

my poetry. What do these tools do to language? One of them repeats a beat, the other one repeats a sound: they both set up repeating patterns. Patterns—in writing, in a carpet, in a fern-head – give the onlooker a sense of understanding and prediction. Rhyme and rhythm are as simi tar a's nails and screws. They do the same thing in different ways.

Using too much rhyme and rhythm will carve away a poem until nothing is left except patterns. People desire patterns to be perfect. But people also desire art to be imperfect. A poet who wants all rhyme and rhythm to be flawless is working on patterns instead of poetry.

Desire for symmetry and desire for asymmetry compete in the reader. The balanced shape of a crucifix is plainly beautiful. But a perfectly beautiful face is perfectly dull: the living asymmetry of an oak leaf is delightful. The Japanese ceramic, Navajo weaving and the mediaeval music of Abbess Von Hildegard are made beautiful by intentional lack of balance— the perfect circle of a tea-bowl is indented, the carpet has one unfinished thread, the music has one humanising discordance. There are correlations of this in poetry—in my poetry—in half-rhyme and broken rhythm.

At the end of the day these are only equipment – linseeds and turpentines, not the poetry itself. I think or poetry itself as a much odder animal, not one to be picked up by the flanges and examined in an essay. But there was a CD player advertisement on the Tube this morning showing a goosepimple magnified 500 times. I know I want my poetry to do that.

First published in the *PBS Bulletin*, Autumn 1996.

Index of Poem Titles

Amphibians	229
A Bowl of Green Fruit	244
A Crossroads	170
The Barber's Daughter	64
The Beekeepers	115
Broken Bone	100
The City of Clocks	72
Close	11
Closing Time	132
Doctor Crippen in Love	149
Dowsing with Whalebones	166
Draining the Grand Union	122
Dreaming of Home	49
Drunk Autumn Midnight below Victoria Embankment	144
Earthquake, Osaka 1995	84
The Elephant Girl	130
Excerpts from a London Zoo Guide Book, 1928	162
Five Ways of Looking at my Grandfather	232
Flora & Fauna	143
Flora and the Admiral	91
From the Bullet Train	52
From the Diaries of Henry Morgan, Summer 1653	189
Gibbons in a Northern Spring	137
The Gifts	223
Gravity	222
Green Tea Cooling	56
Homesickness	80
Horse Chestnuts	247
How to Curse	138

How to Light Dynamite	89
In the Rooms of the Plague House	17
Introduction	1
The Island of Pumpkins	164
Jael	58
July 14th, 10 p.m.	114
Leonardo's Machines	134
Life Savings	108
The Lighthouse Keeper's Cat	230
Lime Light	151
The Long Road to Silence	62
London Pastoral	9
Love Song	98
Magnolia Flowers	121
Makondi Sculpture	68
Meat	112
Michael the Zoo Keeper	128
Midnight in the City of Clocks	117
The Mosquito's Opposite	13
The Mule and the Rain	87
New Verses for Clock City Magpies	95
Nine in the Morning in the Station Bar	241
A Night in the Room of the Clown	160
Nightlight	184
Night-Ride, Japan	40
The Nightworkers	224
Nocturne	252
North-West London, 8.15	96
A Note on the Text	ix
One Day in Hiroshima	77

On the Island of Pearls	42
On the Slow Mountain Train	54
The Orator	226
A Page of a Guide to a Small Island	168
The Patron Saint of Prisoners	145
The Pilot in Winter	179
Playground at 2 a.m.	101
Playing Japanese Chess with the Elder Mrs Uchida	81
Poem for a North London Wedding	153
Prelude	50
Prisons in a Departure Lounge at Midnight	75
Prospero's Cell	147
Reasons Why	110
Repossession	191
The Ritual of Making	66
Rio in Carnival	46
Saturday Night Fever	158
The Secret of Burning Diamonds	19
Self-Portraits by Children	156
Sheep's Clothing	102
Snake Oil	38
Snapshot of an Egotist	155
The Sound of Cages	177
Sumo Wrestler in Sushi Bar	83
Summer Late Night Opening	249
Sushi	126
Synthesis	220
Three Wishes in a Small Town	85
To a Boy on the Underground	195
Today the House is Full of Dishcloths	44

Transit	74
TV Dinner	219
Twelfth Night	124
The Vampire's Price	60
Waiting	15
The Wave	245
The Woman who Talks to Ezra Pound in Tesco	106
The Woman Who Likes Standing Under Trees in the Rain	239
Xenophobia	104
A Year in Japan	21
A Year in London	196
Yellow	243

Index of First Lines

After eight days the fall eases.	28
After the alarm,	175
After the death of his middle son,	235
After work he feeds the wolves	149
All day it lies as if extinct,	230
All day the hills smell of sawdust.	85
All night she keeps the car radio on,	243
All night, the smell of greasepaint	160
Along the jetty, sparrows nag	42
Always three steps ahead	38
And as the years passed	50
And so on May Day's eve I came to London,	189
And sometimes months go by when London	213
And the sky wet as a loose tarpaulin.	144
April, and this year April is	117
At six my rooms shake when the train	23
At the far edge	52
Before morning I'm waiting here,	15
Between the ebb of dusk	81
Between the leather seats	54
Between the rag-slap of docks	31
Beyond the rocks of Ephesus	49
Beyond the rocks of Ephesus	80
Bought from the marts of Amsterdam	19
By the subway exit	35
Cutting into colour,	220
Don't get me wrong. Your face is smooth and soft	102
Each night, the headlights of his car	237
Eight for black, nine for white.	95
Ever since summer blew their candles out	247

Fishing the warm newspaper off his chips,	223
For my birthday, roast sparrow	24
For ten days there is no weather	132
Full moon tonight	252
Here he is, his face pressed to the glass,	234
Here is Basil Philip's microscope,	232
His mother was a magician at nights,	128
How can there have been a time when this	222
Hungover, and forgetting to bring water,	198
I am a follower of water.	166
I ask for love;	244
I leave with no reason except to walk,	170
I'm the one with seven forks,	155
I've been watching it all day	87
I walk to the hills where the old town is,	180
In the dark	121
In the hills of the Island of Pumpkins	164
In the small hours	126
In the small hours, the first snow	245
It happens quite suddenly,	122
It is a warm winter this year.	124
It's closing time at the bloodmobile.	96
I've been watching it all day	87
Ladies and gentlemen, listen!	60
Late-shift done and only the bike	40
Lock the door. Is it locked?	104
London—there's a rhythm to the name,	216
Long after midnight	224
Look for violence	139
Monday finds him early at his station,	226

Mr Salter walks across the garden like an astronaut;	115
Mr Toumbi's second son, fire slopping from his hand,	89
My favourite memory of him:	238
My god is this whole bloody place	249
No cats out in this weather,	229
Noon. In its sleep the earth turns over	25
Noon. In the public park	56
North London suits them	153
October, and you buy pomegranates,	215
One salmon-egg, a boil or pearl,	83
Only the heartwood	68
Only when the green river	62
Out to the bedroom-towns with their	171
Outside the station,	143
Peace Park. In the postwar trees	77
Promise me something. Promise me	98
Promise me you won't forget,	140
River town. Ghettos of mud	78
Salt fruit on a white plate.	179
She'd like to sleep. Letters of ice	74
She dreams of chess.	131
She forgets her own smell. She tries and can't	130
She has another fall at Christmas.	112
She keeps the knick-knacks clean like fruit	91
She leans the door against a wall.	84
She meets the train	34
She thinks them patchwork—	130
Slaughter-month. The road is down	72
Someone in that house must be in love	207
Spring in the rush-hour train:	26

Such a brilliant weapon	13
Sweat cools to a sheen	29
Take time. Take out the brunt	138
The cockroaches are rain-skittish.	11
The dead worry me.	108
The earth is hot,	46
'The finest cook in the province!'	66
The first chess players have returned,	202
The first we heard of it was the silence.	191
The island cisterns have been dry	168
The laptop cauls your face with light,	195
The man with *Agent of Tai Wing Wa*	75
The moon round as an oven-dial.	114
The newspapers, chained to the rack,	21
The old fishmonger with the cropped grey hair	210
There have been better years.	145
There is subsidence.	151
There's something I've wanted to show you. Here—	9
The street outside jointed with leery boys	204
The tranquillity—	36
The whorehouses and warehouses	147
The woman who likes standing under trees in the rain.	239
The woman who talks to Ezra Pound in Tesco	106
They came away from our mountain wars	58
The Zoological Gardens	162
This is called Kevin.	156
Today the house is full of dishcloths,	44
Today the world is ugly:	100
Under the nightlight	184

Under the rain	137
Under the tin roof he listens	182
Up at 4 a.m. to piss,	200
Waiting for thaw in a thin country	173
Watch this—	110
We're waiting for the light to change	134
We walk each other home	177
What does the man in the old brown suit	241
What else are net curtains for?	101
What frost there was is nearly gone by the time I'm up to look	218
when pigeons like *dei ex machina*	212
When summer comes, no one is left	17
When the cursing is all done	141
With one clean movement	64
Working the clubface	158
You at the counter, cutting onions into moons,	219
You're late, you're late, you're late the blackbird says,	196

This book has been typeset by
SALT PUBLISHING LIMITED
using Sabon, a font designed by Jan Tschichold
for the D. Stempel AG, Linotype and Monotype
Foundries. It has been manufactured using Holmen
Book Cream 65gsm paper, and printed and bound by
Clays Limited in Bungay, Suffolk, Great Britain.

CROMER
GREAT BRITAIN
MMXXVI